Hung Jury

First published 2012
by Transgress Press
Oakland, CA 94608

© 2012 Transgress Press

Library of Congress Cataloging in Publication Data
Hung Jury: testimonies of genital surgery by transsexual men / edited by Trystan T.
Cotten

ISBN: 0-6156-9235-4
ISBN-13: 9780615692357
Library of Congress Control Number: 2012948322
Transgress Press, Oakland, CA

Hung Jury

Testimonies of Genital Surgery by Transsexual Men

Edited by Trystan T. Cotten

Transgress Press
Oakland, CA 94608

Contents

Acknowledgements

Foreword   i
Shannon Minter

The Jury's Still Out   1
Rethinking the Verdict on Female-to-Male Genital Surgery
Trystan T. Cotten

Part I
The Proof's In the Penis

Metoidioplasty   13

A Nice Little Package   15
Keith Josephson

Man to Man   23
Logan Grimes

Transforming to Masculine Embodiment   29
Tone

Hanging On   37
Lou Sullivan's Embodiment of Gay Identity
Brice D. Smith

Phalloplasty   57

One Man's Junk   59
Declan

Somatic Integrity   69
Gabriel Richardson

Before and After   79
Cinque

Transforming from Within   91
Paul James

Success Is the Best Revenge   97
Dr. Hope

A Phoenix's Quest for the Dragon   103
Nickolas J. McDaniel

Phalloplasty Fallacies   111
David E. Weekley

All It Takes is Time and Tramadol   117
John Henry

The First Man-Made Man   127
Pagan Kennedy

A Guided Tour through Phalloplasty   135
Martin Kincaid

Part II
Witnessing Transformation

A Femme's Chrysalis   149
Isabella Abrahams

Fringe Benefits   155
Dr. Laura

Gifts and Talents   159
Deborah Weekley

Out of the Shadows   163
Paula James

Going the Distance   167
Andree Culpepper

Acknowledgements

This book would not have been possible without the contributions and support of many people. First and foremost, I want to thank and praise the contributors for their generosity and openness in sharing their stories so that others may benefit. It takes incredible courage and trust to share private and personal experiences of this kind. I also want to thank Zander Keig for championing this project and playing a vital role from its inception. His enthusiasm, written contributions, and input on book design and promotion were instrumental in bringing the project to fruition. Sandy Shuster deserves much thanks and praise for coming to our rescue in the 11th hour and putting other projects on hold to proof the manuscript. She brought a compassionate perspective and insightful editorial advice. Special thanks also to Alexia Brooks for her editorial assistance. I also want to give warm thanks to Kristine Medea, Brice D. Smith, and Max Valerio for believing in and supporting the project throughout. I am grateful to my femme wife, Isabella Abrahams, for her personal testimony, love, wisdom, and continuing support. There are many others I want to thank, colleagues, friends, and family, whose names I cannot list here. Without their encouragement, love, and support, which sustained and reminded me of the reasons I began this project, this book might have never been completed

Foreword

Shannon Minter

I have a confession to make. During my nearly 20 years of legal advocacy for transgender people, I have often been part of the problem this book is designed to address. Like too many other advocates and community members, I have portrayed genital surgeries for transgender men in overly negative terms. On many occasions, I have said that the quality of the surgery is poor, the appearance and functionality are inadequate, the cost is prohibitive, and the risk of complications is inordinately high. Little wonder, I would often conclude, that most transgender men do not obtain them. I now realize these statements paint only a partial and, in some respects, quite misleading picture.

In my defense, I made these disparaging statements mostly in the context of legal cases where I was desperately trying to defend the rights of transgender men who did not have genital surgery and were at risk of being declared legally female for that reason. In virtually every such case, these men were dragged into court through no choice of their own and forced to defend their legal gender in order to maintain relationships with their children. Often, whether a transgender man can be recognized as a child's legal father will depend on whether he is legally recognized as male. Under the pressure of these circumstances, it seemed important to explain to courts that the quality of FTM surgeries is so poor and the level of risk so high that it would be unreasonable to require a transgender man to undergo them to be recognized as legally male.

For example, in one case, my client was a transgender man fighting to have his marriage declared valid so that he could continue to be a legal parent to his two children, aged 6 and 9. He had transitioned at the age of twenty-one and lived as a man virtually his entire adult life. He had married a woman and raised two children, one adopted and one born through assisted reproduction. When he filed for divorce, his wife challenged the validity of the marriage in order to separate him from the children. My colleagues and I presented expert testimony from a surgeon who was extremely compassionate and dedicated to the wellbeing of transgender people, and who strongly believed that gender identity alone should determine a person's legal sex. To this day, I remain deeply grateful for his genuine respect and concern for transgender people, and his willingness to donate his time free of charge. In retrospect, however, I also realize that, in important respects, he had only a limited—and overly negative—perspective on phalloplasties for transgender men. He described them as, "at best…a tube of skin and meat hanging between their legs." He testified that a constructed phallus cannot function sexually like a penis, is incapable of erection, and has no sensitivity. He stated that he had never seen a phalloplasty that looked like a real penis and that its appearance may worsen over time, so that it becomes "kind of flaccid and wrinkled up [like a] piece of—to me I think it looks like a dried up cucumber."

These statements are difficult to recount, and I do so with genuine remorse and regret for the pain they cause to me and other transgender men. Even if they are accurate in some limited sense about the outcomes of some particular surgical techniques and individual surgeries, they paint with far too broad a brush. They are needlessly harsh and disparaging. They discount the subjective experiences of transgender men. They play into damaging stereotypes of transgender people as freakish and tragic. And they arbitrarily adopt an idealized view of the appearance and functioning of non-transgender men's genitalia as the only measure of success.

I have also made overly negative statements about genital surgeries for transgender men in an effort to stop the enactment of laws or policies that provide access to an appropriate bathroom only to transgender people who have had genital surgery. Almost invariably, legislators and employers initially assume that genital surgery is the only objective test for whether a transgender person is entitled to be recognized in their new gender. Countering that misconception requires a massive educational effort—about the nature and variety of transgender identities, the realities of gender transition, and the absence of any medical basis for using genital surgery as the litmus test of a transgender person's authenticity or entitlement to recognition and respect. In these contexts, I have sometimes fallen back on arguments that genital surgeries for transgender men are inadequate and inordinately risky to help persuade decision makers not to base their restroom policies on genital surgery. In some cases, I have reluctantly used myself as an example, noting that while no employer would want my balding, bearded presence in a women's restroom, I have opted not to obtain genital surgery because I believed the results were inadequate.

My goal in these situations was noble—to secure rights for all transgender people regardless of their surgical status. It is a goal I still passionately support and continually work to achieve. But the means I have used in the past—disparaging the quality and efficacy of genital surgeries for transgender men—were wrong, and I am determined not to rely on those misleading arguments any longer.

To be clear, when I made these arguments, I genuinely believed them to be true, based on the information available at the time. Like so many other transgender men, I had searched in vain for any detailed, accurate, and understandable information about the surgical options available for genital reconstruction. Over the years, as I matured in my own transition, I became increasingly eager to find that information and increasingly frustrated by how difficult it was to obtain. The sources of information I could find were extremely limited. I found a few websites devoted to sharing information about surgeries for transgender men, but to my disappointment, most of them focused on top surgery. Photos and descriptions of genital surgeries were few and far between, and the pictures tended to be taken immediately after surgery, when little healing had taken place. As a result, they were often hard to evaluate.

Despite these difficulties, I was able to find some information, and, over time, my perspective began to shift. For example, one of my clients who had a phalloplasty kindly showed me his surgery. It looked great—nothing at all like what I had been conditioned to expect. He shared as well that he had an active and satisfying sexual life with women, though he was frustrated at not being able to stand and pee. His self-confidence as a man was incredibly heartening, and I can still recall our conversations vividly after more than 15 years. I also had an opportunity to see the phalloplasty of two transgender men from Belgium who generously agreed to do a show and tell at an FTM International meeting in San Francisco. My female partner accompanied me, and I still recall her observation that, as someone who had been intimate with non-transgender men, she would not have been able to tell the difference. Over the years, I have also benefitted enormously from the openness of transgender men such as Jamison Green, who shared their experiences and satisfaction with metoidioplasties, and Loren Cameron, who provided an incredible window into the world of FTM genital surgeries in his book *Body Alchemy: Transsexual Portraits*. In 2011, at the international transgender conference in Barcelona, Spain, I was struck by a conversation I had with another transgender man from Belgium who expressed surprise that so few men in the United States had genital surgery. He conveyed that he was very satisfied with his own phalloplasty and knew many other Belgian trans men who felt the same way.

As I gained more information, I developed a much more positive picture of these surgeries. I started to worry about the message that legal and political advocates—myself included—were communicating to the world. I began to realize that, albeit with the best of intentions, we were presenting a misleading and inaccurate picture that was not only providing false information to courts, policy makers and legislators, but also to other community members.

Once this realization sunk in, I stopped disparaging the genital surgeries available to transgender men and have not done so for several years now. Even now, however, I still catch myself asserting that many transgender men in the U.S. do not need or want genital reconstructive surgery and that the vast majority do not have it. While both of those statements may be true, I believe that making them without providing more of a context is misleading. While some—perhaps even many—transgender men do not need or want genital surgery, many others do. And while many—perhaps even most— transgender men in the U.S. do not obtain genital surgery, we must always be clear that at least part of the reason stems from the daunting obstacles to obtaining genital surgery in this country, including the failure of most public and private health insurance plans to cover the cost. In countries where the costs of genital surgeries are covered, a greater percentage of transgender men choose to have them. Through my own experience as an advocate, I have come to believe that whenever we talk about the number of transgender people in the U.S. who do not have genital surgery, we must acknowledge that many people urgently need and desire to have these surgeries but simply do not have access to them.

In addition, under the present legal and social circumstances in the U.S., I question whether we know the full truth about how many transgender people in this country either have or desire genital surgery. Some national advocacy groups, including my own, have undertaken community surveys showing that high percentages of transgender people—especially transgender men—do not have genital surgery. For example, a 2011 survey by the National Center for Transgender Equality and the National Gay and Lesbian Task Force found that more than 75 percent of transgender women and more than 90 percent of transgender men have not undergone any genital reconstructive surgeries. Increasingly, advocates are relying on this data to argue that anti-discrimination laws and other policies affecting transgender people should not turn on whether a person has had genital surgery, since doing so would exclude so many transgender people from protection. This is a laudable goal, and one that I fully support. At the same time, we must be careful not to over-generalize based on these limited survey results. Almost certainly, these surveys capture a limited segment of our community, and they are particularly unlikely to reach the many transgender men and women who are not connected to LGBT groups and who may be more likely than those who are to have undergone genital reconstructive surgery.

We must acknowledge another truth as well. The tendency of many advocates and community members to be negative about genital surgery cannot be explained solely by a desire to stand up for the rights of those who do not want surgery or cannot afford to have it. There is also a more troubling aspect of this tendency, which speaks to more deeply rooted issues in our psyches and communities. As some of the essays in this volume so poignantly describe, many transgender men suffer from an inordinate amount of misplaced guilt about seeking out medical modification of our bodies—and in particular genital surgery—and many others are quick to judge those who do.

Other factors may be at work as well. When faced with financial and other barriers that seem to place genital surgeries out of reach, we may seek to protect ourselves by devaluing what we cannot have. In addition, because many transgender men have been conditioned to deny our deepest needs, we may believe that we do not deserve genital surgery, or even unconsciously fear that we will be punished if we dare to seek it out.

It is important to acknowledge the many reasons why these negative attitudes exist and to face these issues honestly and forthrightly. It is important for each of us to examine our own attitudes toward genital surgery and to determine, what do, I, as an individual, want and need? Our goal must be to answer that question from a foundation of self-worth and confidence in the legitimacy of our own needs, experiences, and desires. Each of us deserves to feel whole and to feel comfortable with our bodies. We deserve to have a social, sexual, and personal life that is rewarding and satisfying, and that allows us to express—and be—our fullest selves.

The Jury's Still Out: Rethinking the Verdict on Female-to-Male Genital Surgery

Trystan T. Cotten

Many female-to-male trans men pursue genital surgery for numerous reasons.[1] Despite how well testosterone and chest surgery masculinizes our bodies, some trans men are unable to reconcile their sexual anatomy with the rest of their male body and identity. Many feel driven or compelled to change and align our genitals with our gender to feel fully integrated and whole. Genital surgery can also open doors of social bonding and intimacy with others that are inaccessible or feel too risky to pursue without genitals that match our gender presentations, including locker rooms, showers, public baths, health spas, saunas, swimming pools, fraternities, the military, bars (including sex and strip clubs), and circle jerks, to name some. Navigating these spaces can be tricky and scary for trans men whose genitals and personal histories differ from others' assumptions and expectations. Many trans men feel uncomfortable and/or unsafe disrobing in locker rooms and public showers. Being unable to immerse and fully participate in the rituals and practices of these spaces can also feel constraining to some trans men, who may come to feel that they are missing out on valuable experiences and relationships with others.

Genitoplasty also opens up opportunities for romantic and sexual intimacy. It is difficult for some men to face their genitals in the mirror in private, and the prospect of explaining them to a potential lover or someone to whom we are attracted can feel daunting, scary, and even shameful. Founding father of the female-to-male (FTM) trans movement, Lou Sullivan, wrote extensively and eloquently about the challenges he faced as a gay trans man in San Francisco's gay community in the 1980s. Through surgery Sullivan finally came to feel whole and integrated in his body in a long, hard fought journey to be his true self. It also opened up social and sexual connections with other men, allowing him to function and be seen as one of the guys. Many contributors of this collection describe how genital surgery enhanced sexual and emotional intimacy with their partners. When trans people feel more integrated and secure in our bodies (and the world), we are able to bring more of ourselves to relationships and participate more fully. We can open up emotionally and sexually while giving and receiving pleasure more fully.

Safety and security also motivate trans people to seek genital surgery. We are reminded daily of our structural disadvantage and vulnerability to harassment and discrimination. Sometimes we are thrown into difficult circumstances over which we have little control. Traveling across national borders and passing through security check points, we are vulnerable to suspicion, ridicule, and abuse by law enforcement personnel who are not always trained to deal with trans people. Trans cultural lore abounds in stories of people who have been strip-searched, interrogated, and intimidated at security gates. What is more, when trans people are incarcerated, many are assigned to prisons based on genitals rather than gender identity. Having genitals that match our gender presentations can mitigate some of the stress we feel in these situations and encounters.

In addition to safety, somatic congruence, and sexual/social connection, other issues of sovereignty and quality of life also come into play. In some places, including some states in the U.S., genital surgical reconstruction is necessary for changing the gender marker on one's birth certificate and other identity documents. Being deprived of legal gender recognition can have a punitive impact on trans people's lives, affecting our naturalization and citizenship, marriage rights, hospital visitation rights, child custody, divorce settlements, and estate transfers, to name some. Trans people can lose custody rights of children in divorce settlements if the partner chooses to exploit social prejudice and use the trans partner's (unreconstructed) genitals to nullify the marriage (See Shannon Minter's "Foreword.") Trans people can also be jailed and fined for using the "wrong" bathroom when police officers want to exploit the genitally specific legal definition of restrooms. While it is important to change these laws and restrictions, genitoplasty can sometimes prevent trans people from being so ruthlessly victimized.

These issues, trans men's motivations, and the transformative outcomes of genital surgery are rarely treated in commentaries and conversations on the topic. Instead, much of the focus in academic, community, and popular media discourses is more narrowly concerned with aesthetics and functionality and carries a negative tenor and verdict. Some scholars misspeak and perpetuate the myth that FTM genital surgery is unsuccessful and produces aesthetically poor, nonfunctioning penises (Heyes 2009, Noble 2006, Rubin 2003, Jeffries, 2003, Halberstam 1998). These sentiments are echoed in the mainstream media (talk shows, documentaries, movies, and television) as well, and not only miseducate the public about genital surgery, but paint a grim portrait of medical transitioning possibilities for trans male and masculine identified people.

At times, the discourse of genital surgery descends into the verbal gutter where we openly and (seemingly) without reservation describe trans men's penises as "frankendicks," "mangled mutilations," and "insensate sausages." The following is an excellent example from an internet blog: "Finally, there are a couple of surgical procedures that can be done to construct dangly bits. Those are expensive (like you could put your kid through a couple of years of college or buy yourself a really nice car for the money), and depending on which one a guy has, it may not be all that functional or aesthetically pleasing. Imagine if you will a piece of sausage with a drinking straw shoved through it. Now imagine that attached to you."[2] This kind of commentary demeans and trashes trans male's bodies and reinforces dominant cultural ideas of us as freaks who are doomed to tragic lives. Several authors in this collection address this problem and recount how insensitive, uninformed commentary not only hurt them emotionally, but also dissuaded them from pursuing genital surgery.

Blanket pronouncements that genital surgery is unsuccessful are not only false and misleading, but they also imply that trans men's genitalia are inauthentic second-hand replicas of cis-gender men's penises which are implicitly taken as the standard of measurement. (Assumptions about cis-gender men's genitals also seem out of touch with the reality of variation in size, shape, color, and functional capacity among cis-gender men.) Sometimes, we forget that "bodies" are more than just objects of discourse and that they belong to actual people with feelings, desires, and aspirations. Loree Cook-Daniels reminds us that words have a social and emotional impact: "What may be to some of us an abstract, theoretical discussion may be to someone else a very real personal attack."[3]

Double standards abound in the discourse on genital surgery. For one, we compare the surgically modified genitals of trans men to cis-gender males, but refrain from doing this with trans men who have not undergone surgery.

The latter would be criticized as trans phobic, normative, and oppressive. Secondly, rarely do we speak disparagingly of the genitals of cis-gender men or females (trans, cis-gender, or intersex) who have undergone genitoplasty. Not that I am suggesting that we should. However, the point I want to emphasize is that we have a negative, judgmental propensity toward trans men acquiring penises that does not extend to other bodies. Related to this contradiction is a third double standard of treating genitoplasty differently from chest reconstruction. In the eighties and early nineties when FTM transitioning and trans men were becoming more visible, chest surgery was questioned and sometimes disparaged by people who knew little about female-to-male transsexuals and/or imposed a political interpretation on their transition choices. Now chest surgery is largely accepted and rarely questioned. But genital surgery however remains a lightning rod for criticism and "glass-half-empty" thinking.

Much of the criticism of genital surgery is rarely based on current or extensive research, or on personal experience. When I ask critics of FTM genitoplasty for their information source, typically they reply that they heard or read about it somewhere else. It seems that much of the criticism of genitoplasty is born from hearsay and conjecture that play off and echo one another as "evidence" in a discourse that is negatively predisposed against bottom surgery. When a trans man's experience is actually cited, the example is usually dated and does not reflect recent surgical advances made over the last 15 years. Many people still refer to Michael Dhillon, who received the first medically engineered penis (known to date) in 1949 from the well-known British surgeon, Dr. Harold Gillies. Some photographs and testimonies of genital surgery posted on websites also contribute to misconceptions of genital surgery. Many portfolios of penises are still in progress and do not include information or images of the final results. Some photos were taken immediately after surgery when the genitals were bruised and swollen, and still healing from complications and infections. These penises are still in the midst of a multistage process with more surgeries scheduled in the future. Some photographs are also dated, over ten years old, and do not reflect recent advancements in surgical techniques and technologies. The few images posted on the internet are by no means representative of tens of thousands of surgically modified genitals of trans men. Making disparaging comments about trans male bodies, however, discourages many men from sharing their surgical experiences and results. Incomplete and dated surgical outcomes posted on the internet work in conjunction with the treatment of hearsay and conjecture as fact to produce and perpetuate myths and misinformation of FTM genitoplasty.

While I like to encourage critical discussion and numerous perspectives on any subject matter, the question of whether genital surgery is successful is probably answered best by those who have some first-hand experience. This applies to physicians also. Medical genius combined with decades of trans activism have made options of medical transitioning more available to trans people, but medical experts are not infallible. Like academics, doctors and healthcare providers sometimes misspeak. If they do so, it is usually for several reasons. First, their knowledge may be based on their own limited experience with patients who want them to correct another surgeon's work. These samples are small, too small, to generalize about all trans men's experiences with genital surgery. What is more, doctors performing corrective surgeries rarely see or hear from trans men who have good surgical experiences and are happy with their results.

Sometimes surgeons misspeak about genital surgery because of the gap or time lag between their textbook understanding of human anatomy and physiology and our trans bodies that are being rewired by surgeons. Genital surgical reconstruction is a complex, multistage process involving cutting, splicing, pulling, tucking, and transplanting bundles of nerves, arteries, blood vessels, skin, fat and muscle from one area of the body to another to take up new residences and functions and offer trans people new somatic and sentient experiences. Surgery rewires our erotic circuitry and urinary tract, which requires learning how to use and relate to again. Thus, transitioning bodies are not only rewriting normative scripts of sex and gender, but they are also rewriting medical knowledge of human anatomy, physiology, and surgical practice, as surgeons continue experimenting with new practices and technologies to produce better results for their patients. These advancements are reported in the medical literature, which presents a more nuanced and positive portrait of FTM genital surgery, but some doctors are not abreast of these reports. Hence, a physician's knowledge of what is (and is not) possible for FTM genitoplasty can lag behind the actual practice of genital modification and the new sentient and somatic experiences it opens up for trans bodies.

The negative verdict on genital surgery is premature and misinforms the public, adversely affecting trans men who need accurate information. Transgender medicine is a broad and rapidly developing multidisciplinary field. New developments and breakthroughs in medical knowledge, surgical techniques, and technology are occurring every year. Surgical outcomes depend on a variety of factors including: the surgeon's skill and experience; the patient's genital configuration; his medical history, immune system, and genetics (including racially and ethnically specific medical conditions, disorders, and healing tendencies); his diet, nutrition and exercise habits; postoperative hygiene practices and environment; and the patient's stress level and emotional well-being. All these factors combine in ways that are unique and specific to each person, affecting everyone's healing and surgical outcomes differently. Thus, it is difficult (and perhaps impossible) to make objective generalizations about the results of FTM genital surgery. Subjective anecdotal accounts by trans men who have experienced surgery are just as useful and reliable sources of knowledge as the speculative guessing of those without experience.

Notable exceptions in the discourse of FTM genital surgery include: Aaron Devor's *FTM: Female-to-Male Transsexuals in Society* (1997), Jay Prosser's *Second Skins: The Body Narratives of Transsexuality* (1998), Loren Cameron's *Man Tool: The Nuts and Bolts of Female-to-Male Surgery* (2001), and Dean Kotula's, *Phallus Palace: Female to Male Transsexuals* (2002). These authors go beyond aesthetics and functionality and present a more balanced profile of the motivating factors and outcomes of genitoplasty for trans men. Devor and Prosser treat genital surgery from the perspective of transitioning subjects themselves. Cameron and Kotula feature photographic representations and short autobiographical vignettes of both chest and genital surgical reconstruction.

Hung Jury continues these efforts to educate and enlighten readers about FTM genitoplasty. The collection puts a human face and flesh on the discourse of FTM genital surgery and enables better understanding and appreciation of trans men's journeys. The testimonies present a more balanced and in depth understanding of the ups and downs of our surgical experience, how we cope, and how it affects our lives. Nineteen contributors, trans men and their partners, share the surgical, social, sexual, somatic, spiritual, and psychological dimensions of surgery's transformative impact on their lives. They address and challenge many myths of FTM genital surgery with first-hand experience, knowledge, and medical facts. Contributors dispute the notion that metoidioplasty produces small penises incapable of penetration, or that phalloplasty results in insensate penises with no erectile or voiding capacities. They dispel other myths that free flap forearm phalloplasty produces a more sensate penis than other phalloplasty procedures.

Another misleading myth that has sprung up in the last decade is the false division between phalloplasty and metoidioplasty as mutually exclusive surgeries, which leads to further belief that trans men must choose one or the other. Testimonies in this collection challenge these assumptions. In an informative blog, trans man Zerk problematizes this mythic binary and the negative impact of withholding vital knowledge about genitoplasty from trans men considering it.[4] We tend to "organize community discussions, online chat groups, list serves, conference workshops, and our own personal process" into two mutually exclusive tracks of phalloplasty or metoidioplasty. However, he points out ways that many genital reconstruction procedures for trans men share important commonalities like urethraplasty, scrotoplasty, vaginectomy, hysterectomy, clitoral release, prosthetic implants, and skin grafting. Regardless of which surgical path trans men choose, Zerk reminds us that sharing rather than dividing knowledge and experience empowers us to make more informed decisions, take better care of ourselves, and optimize surgical results. Doctors share medical knowledge and surgical techniques and so should trans people.

Hung Jury hopes to raise the level of cultural awareness of FTM genital surgery and self-reflexivity of how we talk and write about the topic. The preoccupation with aesthetics and functionality prevents appreciation for trans men's journeys, what we endure, and genitoplasty's significance for our gender identity and embodiment. Even men who have partial sensation, erectile, or voiding challenges still tend to be happy with their penis, and more importantly, their bodies and themselves and rarely regret having surgery. While aesthetics and functional proximity to non-trans male penises are important ideals to some trans men, authors in this collection reveal more extensive and complex motivations for seeking surgery, and surgical outcomes that are more positive and rewarding than critics portray. In addition, we hope that this book will contribute to shifting the way FTM genital surgery is discussed to a more informed and respectful discourse. Moving in this direction may require that we position ourselves when discussing the topic and identify our involvement and experiences with bottom surgery.

Authors in this collection write about their own feelings and experiences and do not intend to suggest that acquiring a penis should be the final goal of FTM gender transitions, or that gender transitions are incomplete without a penis. Nor do contributors intend to imply that a penis is essential to a person's male identification, or the sole measure of male identity or manliness. While editing this collection, I frequently encountered the phallocentric myth that trans men would choose genitoplasty if it were more affordable and accessible. I expected this reaction from people who had never learned to question the sex/gender binary or heteronormativity, but I was surprised to hear it from my fellow trans, queer, and feminist friends. I want to take a moment to address this assumption. Thousands of trans men have undergone genitoplastic reconstruction, and truthfully, many more would have the surgery if it was covered by medical insurance or cost less. But many trans men are also happy with their vaginas—renamed and re-conceived as "manholes" and "dick/clits" by some trans men—and would never dream of changing them, because they are comfortable with their genitals, get immense sexual pleasure, and don't feel that their manhood is diminished. Jody Helfand writes movingly of his self-acceptance and joy: "I'm finally admitting that I don't mind having a vagina. Why does it matter if I feel pleasure there? It doesn't have to be defined as 'female' pleasure; pleasure is pleasure, and I don't need to label or define my pleasure based on gender.... I have a masculine, male vagina with an enlarged two inch clit that gets thick and hard and can get sucked—that can go inside a woman the way a thumb would. I can have sex with my enlarged clit/dick, and when I do it, my vagina gets wet...The truth is that I enjoy my vagina. It's a source of pleasure for me, and I'm finally able to admit this and have fun with it. My vagina is masculine. It's aggressive and powerful. It takes charge and control, and dominates. I'm proud of my vagina. And why does the word 'vagina' have to be associated with only women, anyway?"[5]

The testimonies gathered here also offer valuable insight into the relationship of bodily materiality to gender identity and expression and the social, psychological, somatic, and sexual changes of medical transitions. Predominant focus on the social construction and performativity of gender/sex/sexuality in gender theory tends to ignore and leave unexplored questions about sex morphology and the role of flesh and fluids in gender identity and embodiment (Coogan 2007). Authors in this anthology discuss in detail what the fleshly specificity of having (and not having) a penis means for their gender embodiment and expression. Some men can work through the contradictions posed by their genitals. For others, however, the chasm is too great and formidable to overcome, so we turn to surgery to reconfigure our morphological sex.

These heartfelt testimonies offer a compelling argument for comprehensive medical insurance covering FTM genitoplasty. While surgery is essential for many trans men, it is prohibitively expensive and unattainable for most. In the United States genital surgery can range anywhere from three- to a hundred-thousand dollars and more, depending on the type of surgery, the surgeon's fees, hospitalization, travel, post-operative care needs, and recovery, which can also be costly if surgery prevents one from returning to work. In other countries with national health care plans such as Canada, Serbia, Holland, France, and UK, surgery can be less expensive than the U.S., depending on currency exchange rates. Some inroads in the battle for insurance coverage have already been made, as many private, governmental, and non-profit employers are now including transition-related healthcare coverage in their employee benefits plans. Some trans men have also successfully sued insurance companies and Medicaid to win coverage. Social advocacy, education, and market forces are combining, moreover, to make genital surgery increasingly (albeit slowly) more affordable to trans people. Still, much progress remains to be made. Doctors, clinicians, and health service workers can play a major role in convincing insurance providers and employers to cover all sex reassignment surgeries for trans people. In recognition of the many problems faced by trans people procuring health care coverage, Transgress Press is donating a portion of the profit of this book's sales to organizations that help fund and make gender confirming surgeries more affordable for increasing numbers of trans people.

Endnotes

1   Genital surgery for trans men refers to a range of procedures, including hysterectomy, oophorectomy, vaginectomy/colpectomy, scrotoplasty, urethraplasty, metoidioplasty, and phalloplasty. For this book, we are referring specifically to procedures that modify external genitalia.

2   http://theadventuresoftransman.wordpress.com/2012/01/29/aint-no-bodys-business-but-my-own/. Accessed February 5, 2012.

3   http://www.forge-forward.org/handouts/feminismFTM.php.   Accessed December 3, 2011.

4   http://www.youtube.com/watch?v=fzjtTqEJrKs. Accessed August 15, 2011.

5   http://www.jodyrosehelfand.com/apps/blog/show/6451865.   Accessed Jan 20, 2012

Works Cited

Cameron, Loren. 2001. *Mantool: The Nuts & Bolts of Female-to-Male Surgery.* http://www.lorencameron.com/mantool/.

Coogan, Kelly. 2006. "Fleshly Specificity: (Re)considering Transsexual Sub-jects in Lesbian Communities." In ed. Angela Pattatucci Aragon, *Challenging Lesbian Norms: Intersex, Transgender, Intersectional, and Queer Perspectives.* New York: Routledge.

Devor, Aaron. 1997. *FTMs: Female-to-Male Transsexuals in Society.* Blooming-ton, IN: Indiana UP.

Halberstam, Judith. 1998. *Female Masculinity.* Chapel Hill, NC: Duke Uni-versity Press.

Heyes, Cressida J. 2009. "Changing Race, Changing Sex: The Ethics of Self-Transformation." In ed. Laurie Schrage, *"You've Changed": Sex Reassign-ment and Personal Identity.* New York: Oxford UP.

Jeffries, Sheila. 2003. *Unpacking Queer Politics: A Lesbian Feminist Perspective.* Oxford, UK: Polity Press.

Kosla, Dhillon. 2004. *Both Sides Now: One Man's Journey through Womanhood*

Kotula, Dean. 2002. *The Phallus Palace: Female to Male Transsexuals.* Los An-geles: Alyson Publications.

Noble, Jean Bobby. 2006. *Sons of the Movement: FTMs Risking Incoherence on a Post-Cultural Landscape.* Canadian Scholars' Press.

Prosser, Jay. 1998. *Second Skins: Body Narratives of Transsexuality.* New York: Columbia UP.

Rubin, Henry. 2003. *Self-Made Men: Identity and Embodiment among Transsexual Men.* Nashville, TN: Vanderbilt UP.

Part I

THE PROOF'S IN THE PENIS

Metoidioplasty

A form of genitoplasty for trans men, metoidioplasty has been around at least 35 years. It was popularized in the 1970s in the United States by Dr. Donald Laub as an alternative to phalloplasty, which operated under the guise of constructing a phallus to fill a void. In contrast to phalloplasty, metoidioplasty was designed to build upon tissue that already existed, the clitoris (viewed as a homologous to cis-gender male penises), and enhance its resemblance to cis-sexual male genitalia. The surgery takes advantage of testosterone's masculinization of the clitoris and frees the hormonally enhanced organ by detaching the suspensatory ligament holding it in place from the pubic bone, so that the penis may protrude more prominently from the groin area. Other procedures sometimes performed with metoidioplasty are hysterectomy, oophorectomy, vaginectomy, scrotoplasty, urethraplasty, and mons resection, all of which are usually optional. A mons resection is done sometimes to remove fatty tissue from the pubis mons to enhance penile protrusion and increase access to it. Metoidioplasty does not rule out the possibility of having phalloplasty later. In fact, freeing the suspensatory ligaments of the clitoris is usually included in phalloplasty, and some men go on to pursue phalloplastic constructions subsequently after having metoidioplasty.

The cultural lore of metoidioplasty is that it produces penises that are too small or short for penetration and ultimately unsatisfactory for sexual intercourse. The first section of testimonies challenges this thinking. Size and length of metoidioplasty penises vary among trans men and depend on a range of factors. Genetic endowment is one, as some men have large clitorises before transitioning. But also, the combination of hormones, pumping the organ with a device, and directly applying special DHT cream can and does enhance penile length and girth for some men. Many men can masturbate and penetrate with metoidioplasty penises. Because the penile nerve bundles are hormonally enhanced and made more accessible through metoidioplasty, sexual orgasms tend to be more intense and electrifying than before surgery.

A Nice Little Package

Keith Josephson

I was 40 when I decided to transition, although I had contemplated it for decades. That year, I had top surgery, started testosterone, changed my documents, and moved to a different state. I was finally living and working as a man, and enjoying the privacy and anonymity of being stealth. Each logistical step brought me closer to a sense of simple wholeness and rightness. I had waited 40 years to finally be seen as a man and to live what felt like *my* life. Lower surgery was the next step toward righting the balance. It took a while to accept the paradox that all this complicated medical intervention was the path to simplicity and coherence.

Now, looking back ten years after surgery, the anxieties, obstacles, and achievements of transition have faded into distant memory. Before and during the various stages of transition, all the logistical, bureaucratic, and medical tasks seemed endless and overwhelming. It was exciting to cross each step off the list: change name, change documents, change chemistry, change body parts. It feels good to tell this story now. There aren't a lot of places where anyone really needs to know about my build-a-package story. Even given the inevitable pain, blood and recovery time, it was a positive experience. For me, there really is no downside; I have no regrets.

My brain is wired to have a dry, closed, heavy sensation in my crotch; my neurons expect the weight of free-hanging external genitalia. It is a visceral, kinesthetic need to have the body parts that my brain is wired for. Not having the right feedback from my own body was constantly disturbing and distracting. I wanted to feel right. I really hated the sensation—I don't even like saying the words now—of an open wet genital area. It just felt wrong, like well, like nothing else.

My main motivation for surgery was my own desire for completeness, but others' perceptions also played a role. Although few people see me naked, I wanted the confidence of appearing as male as possible. I have what you think I'm supposed to have. I like being able to tell a doctor that I have a nice little package. I'm proud of it. I didn't want to be in an emergency medical situation with female parts. I feel freer to travel now; there's less to explain if I get in an accident and end up in a foreign hospital. I still worry about catheterization if necessary; if I'm unconscious, I hope medical personnel will figure it out.

It's a funny world, this topsy-turvy through-the-looking-glass experience of shape-shifting. I'm well-hung for an FTM, though on the small end of the spectrum for non-trans men. My bulge is barely visible, and I am self-conscious about that to an extent, even though I got what I wanted. Though I don't spend much time in locker rooms, I can be naked in one and look unambiguously male.

The time I chose to do it was a good time in my life to take on a big project. I was three years into transition, had accomplished many goals and was living peacefully as male. My life was coming together and moving forward in a way it hadn't before. I had emerged from financial burdens I acquired in my misguided detour into home ownership and trying to live happily ever after as a lesbian. I now had a girlfriend, and my professional life was taking shape since I could confidently present a male persona. My girlfriend was a supportive helper, travel partner, and motel nurse. She was extremely happy with the results of my surgery. My family had already adjusted to my transition and been supportive during my top surgery, so bottom surgery wasn't so strange for them. If it was, they knew their job was to be positive and keep their judgments to themselves. My mother, who stayed with me after chest surgery, also took care of me after bottom surgery and even accompanied me to Arizona for a revision the following year. I had some worries about the medical risks, but I trusted my surgeon, and he thought that I was well-configured for a good outcome because testosterone had enhanced my naturally good-sized endowment. Dr. Toby Meltzer and his staff were always kind, responsive and helpful by phone, even while they were moving his practice from Oregon to Arizona.

Nuts and Bolts

Since I'd waited so long, I decided to go for the whole shootin' match and get everything done. I was on the table for eight hours. I had a hysterectomy, oophorectomy, vaginectomy, metoidioplasty, mons resection (removal of some fat and skin from the pubis and movement of my package up and forward), and scrotoplasty with expanders (which gradually stretched the scrotal skin to accommodate the testicular implants). I didn't really consider any other procedure. Phalloplasty seemed too complicated and involved too much grafting and scarring. Size was less important to me than retaining sexual sensation and a natural look. I also decided not to mess with the urinary tract. Sitting to pee is the only daily reminder that I don't have standard equipment, but being able to stand at a urinal is just not a big deal for me. The gynecological surgeon did his part first. Hysterectomy and oophorectomy are fairly routine procedures but vaginectomy is bloodier, which makes it riskier and more expensive. I was required to bank my own blood ahead of time for transfusion to offset blood loss in surgery. The surgeon removed the blood-rich vaginal tissues through abdominal incision from inside; I conceived of the procedure like coring an apple, from top to bottom. Then Dr. Meltzer did the genital reconstruction. I spent three nights in the hospital. In the wee hours of the final night, I called the airline from my hospital bed, afraid I wouldn't be able to make the flight the next day. I couldn't reschedule, so I crossed my fingers and somehow rallied for the trip home, which included race-walking with my girlfriend through O'Hare Airport to make a flight connection, clutching my opiates and ice packs.

Reflections on the Process

Although the details of pain, expense, inconvenience and uncertainty seem like ancient history, it was a long haul. A very long haul. I took six weeks off from work to recover and was glad I did. Though I have a high tolerance for pain, there was intense internal pain from the vaginectomy. Coring that apple was brutal. For the first month I lay on the couch watching a lot of TV, using a lot of ice packs, and glad to be taking opiates. Worse than the surgical pain was getting explosive diarrhea from a bug I picked up after my healthy intestinal flora were wiped out by the routine post-surgery antibiotics. After a day or two of phone calls back and forth to Dr. Meltzer and a trip to the lab with a stool sample (thanks, Mom), I got a prescription for another antibiotic that knocked it out.

I also had intense night sweats for the first week or so, going through five or six t-shirts a night. Another call to Oregon and Dr. Meltzer prescribed a week of a low-dose female hormone. The pharmacist was concerned, "Does your son know this is a *female* hormone?" she asked my mother. But it was a good thing and eased the transition. When the swelling began to go down and I dared to look under the dressings, I had a few days of horror and regret. Things didn't look the way I expected and I had a temporary grieving period. Dr. Meltzer was kind and reassuring on the phone, telling me that time and gravity would work their magic, and it would be okay. And, as the months went on, it was.

I was taking short walks outside during the first week, driving after two weeks, and feeling pretty strong after four. Taking off two more weeks after that was important for consolidating my strength. I'm not one of those guys who thinks it's manly to rush back to work. I needed to stay in the cave and honor my dick and balls, since I'd gone to such trouble to get them. This is a big bio-psycho-social event, and I wanted to digest the changes and let my brain and body concentrate on healing.

Pumping the expanders was tedious and painful. At the time of my surgery in 2001, the expander technology involved little sacs connected by tubes to quarter-sized ports implanted under the skin of the pubic mound. I needed to inject 5 to 10 milliliters of saline into each port every week or two for a couple of months. I tried to do this myself a few times, but couldn't see what I was doing well enough. I made weekly trips to my primary care doctor who had never done it before, but she got the hang of it. She also kindly adjusted her rates for these visits, since insurance wasn't going to cover them. I understand there are alternatives to the ports now, which is good, since they were uncomfortable and itchy. On one occasion, I got an infection at the port site. It swelled up and I had a fever. Of course I was going on vacation to the beach that week. I got antibiotics which cleared up the infection, but they were the kind that caused sun sensitivity. I found out the hard way and got a nasty sunburn, felt crappy and spent a lot of time under an umbrella. Lesson: read all package inserts and warnings.

One of the ports wasn't working, and after weeks of trying to fill it and a few calls to Oregon, Dr. Meltzer said that he'd fix it when he inserted the implant on the other side. At the time, this seemed to extend the process endlessly, adding four more months to the timeline. I was ready for this all to be *done,* and it wasn't easy to be patient, thinking about another trip, more money, asking for more time off from work, another surgery and another recovery. The port was upside down, so Dr. Meltzer replaced it (he thought it had flipped over when I was swollen post-surgery). My doctor and I spent another few months pumping the second expander, which went more smoothly and was less painful than the first side. A year later I had some relatively minor revisions; Dr. Meltzer redid the resection to bring things up and forward, and adjusted the scrotum to help the implants sit side by side.

I didn't like being in limbo for close to a year. It was like living in a house that's under construction—something I had done years earlier—wondering when it all would be over, while obsessing over every nail and floorboard. I didn't like being dependent on a medical process to feel normal, and wasn't sure what the final result would be. I had delayed transition until I was 40, partly because I didn't like handing myself over to doctors. Nine months—though a poetic period of gestation—was a long haul from the initial surgery to the final testicular implant, a long time to be in patient mode (in both senses of the word) with ports under my skin, doing wound care, infusions, and being hyper-aware of being medicalized. I just kept envisioning the end of it all and tried to make the best of it. When I had to go to Portland, Oregon I was able to visit with a good friend who lives there, and in Scottsdale, Arizona I found a nice, inexpensive motel with good breakfasts and a poolside happy hour.

I got very tired of talking to doctors about trans stuff and to transguys about doctors. I was tired of life revolving around surgery and tired of being vague about it at work—I was stealth and wanted to keep it that way—when the logistics and recovery were so demanding and distracting. I was ready to have a life with ordinary pleasures and adventures. I couldn't ride a bike—my main form of workout—for a year. But my patience paid off and the unpleasant parts are distant memories now.

The general assumption or stereotype about lower surgery is that it's not worth doing. Wrong! I'm happy with the look, feel, and function of my little package. It's all mine and all natural, with the exception of inert silicone implants, which one of my brothers has too, after a bout with testicular cancer. My equipment works great sexually, and unlike factory-installed models, it can have multiple orgasms. I'm able to get inside vaginally, which works best with the woman sitting on top, and while I can't go deep, women are most sensitive around the vaginal opening, so we can both get enough stimulation to have fun and satisfaction that way. And orally—well, it's good to get a blowjob and have a girlfriend that likes doing it. I always knew what that would feel like. My brain always knew the sensation but now I could feel it in my cock. With or without surgery, my brain was wired for a genital structure that gets stuck inside other things, not one that gets inserted into.

I haven't had a chance to test out my package with someone new for a while. My relationship ended for unrelated reasons, and I've been mostly in "monk mode" for a few years. Oddly enough—maybe a combination of aging, relationship burnout, and career focus—I'm not desperate to hook up. I've never had such a long period of voluntary and happy singleness, and I've needed this time to focus on myself after 25 years of putting a lot of energy into relationships. I'm dating a little now, but being stealth, I have to deal with how and when to out myself. I've been meeting women online, and if email and phone calls go well, meeting up with them in real time. If there's chemistry on the first date, then I can out myself. I don't need to tell them if there's no interest in getting naked. An email after the first or second date is my preferred method. I can say what I want, and she can have her reaction privately and respond when she's ready. If my being trans is too "out there" for her, I don't take it personally. There are many more ordinary things that are deal breakers for me, like someone who wants to get married, have children, or even live together.

Words of Wisdom

If you want lower surgery, are healthy enough and can put together the resources, go for it. You only get one life. Research your options, choose your surgeon carefully, and make sure you have good support. It's essential to have someone to keep you company, advocate for you, chase down the med nurse, and help with the tedium of the medical world, traveling and healing. Taking good care of yourself pre- and post-surgery is key to minimizing complications. Think positive, eliminate stresses, take off enough time from work, and pay attention to nutrition and exercise. Use your brain like an athlete in training: Visualize the results you want, direct attention and intention to your body and what needs to happen. I was able to get disability benefits from the state during my recovery and didn't need to document a lot to do that legally. My contributions paid for that benefit and I was out for a legitimate "abdominal surgery," even if health insurance didn't cover it. This is worth looking into; you might be able to get similar benefits.

Give yourself time to digest and absorb what's happening. This is ostensibly an extreme external makeover, but it is also an inward journey, a private process. I was not just doing some middle-aged plumbing repairs, which is how I vaguely worded it to co-workers at the time. It's a big goal, like the rest of transition or any other major creative achievement, and there is a letdown when each phase is over. You get used to being in training, preparing and recovering. Returning to mundane reality was a relief, but I wasn't used to stasis and not having a big project.

There are also ways to do some self-enhancement to prepare for surgery and to follow up with pumping and skin stretching techniques once the wounds have fully healed. Dr. Meltzer says he's seen obvious growth in guys who pump. It makes sense that the more you stimulate blood flow in the area, the more you feed the nerves and tissues. A simple shoelace (the soft puffy athletic kind of laces) makes a great adjustable cock-ring-like loop that can, for short periods of time, be wrapped and weighted around your cock and balls in various creative arrangements in order to stretch the skin. Has my life changed dramatically since bottom surgery? Not really. Not like it did after top surgery and testosterone. But I can breathe easier, and I have more energy to pursue other goals. Doing something this big reinforces my conviction that I'm the captain of my own ship; I can conquer obstacles and make things happen.

Man to Man

Logan Grimes

Since my earliest memories I have always had a strong sense of myself as male. It was more than just being masculine or tomboyish. I knew that my *place* was among men. I was old enough to know the difference between male and female bodies, and that my own body was not exactly right for my male identity. As a child, I had hoped that my body would develop and grow a penis, but of course that never happened. As a teenager my body was fairly masculine. I had an athletic build and was involved in many sports, and I didn't have feminine curves. This was satisfying for a while but changed later as I got older. Having an athletic build was nice, but I also noticed that my male friends' bodies were continuing to develop further than mine. Their bodies were becoming more muscular and dense while mine remained lean and lighter. Sometimes I would listen to them talking about their sexual journeys and escapades with girls, and I thought of how that would never be possible for me—not in the same way. I felt stifled in my body as a result.

I had developed nicely to a certain point and had a boyish appeal. But I knew that my body would never develop into that of a man. I was not sexually deprived of relationships with women, however. I found plenty of women to date. Interestingly, all the women I dated considered themselves to be either straight or bi. What I missed was women seeing and interacting with me as male—as a man. I wanted a male physique and physical strength. I was a competitive person. I competed with guys a lot, but that is where I felt like my body always betrayed me because I could only compete to a certain point. If I just had that male physique, I felt like I could keep up with the other guys. I did not think too much about not having a penis because I tried to stay in the moment. It might have crossed my mind now and then, but I was trying to live within the bounds of my reality at the time.

I dated girls and explored my sexuality, which sufficed for a while, but by 19 years old, I had begun to realize that I was transsexual rather than lesbian. I saw a transsexual man on "The Phil Donahue Show" who had transitioned from female and was living in the world just fine. He seemed to be happy and content with himself. It made me think about transitioning. For the first time I realized that I could change my body to look and feel like the man I had always felt like internally.

I never identified as a lesbian, but it was the closest category that fit my experiences at the time. When I saw the transsexual man on Donahue's talk show, however, the puzzle finally started coming together. Seeing those other guys meant that I could also transition. Yet, I waited and did not transition right away. Looking back, I realize that race was one of the reasons that I decided to wait. While the transsexual men on the talk show made me aware of the possibility of transitioning, they were also white and I am black. I had never heard of anyone transitioning in the black community, which made it difficult to move forward. I had no idea who to talk to or where to start. I thought about whether I could go on living in my body or not and decided it was bearable at the time.

As I got older, I began thinking how I did not want to live the rest of my life and then die in a female body. So I revisited my options for transitioning. It wasn't until after I had become more financially stable and independent in my thirties that I started thinking about transitioning again. While I was concerned about my birth family's reaction, I felt that I deserved to live a whole and complete life. I was willing to risk losing their support and our connection if that was what it required. Moving forward to transition became more urgent when I met my (current) wife, and once I knew that she would continue loving me as male, I knew I could deal with however my family reacted.

I began physically transitioning at 39. I moved swiftly to change everything while starting hormones. While healing from top surgery, I began researching surgeons who performed bottom surgery. I had seen a few surgical outcomes a decade earlier and was not impressed. As much as I wanted my penis, I tabled the issue and learned to be content with the progress I had made already.

I reconsidered bottom surgery when I realized one day how uncomfortable I felt in my body because the lower half did not match my upper half. I was male from the waist up and could not identify with my body from the waist down. It didn't fit or feel right. I had to explore surgical options to make my body more consistent from head to toe. When I first began testosterone, I felt free and joyful—so free that I had not realized the depth of anguish I felt all those years.

That free feeling happened again after top surgery. I never loathed or disassociated from my body before transitioning. Nor did I have any particular sexual hang-ups about allowing my partners to touch my genitals. After having top surgery, however, I compared how I felt in my skin before and after surgery. My comfort level was immensely different—not even close. It was like peeling off the layers of an onion, allowing the man I had always been to materialize. With each big step I felt increasingly more comfortable in my skin. I can project *all* of who I am now. I love myself more now. It is not that I did not love myself before. I have always had integrity and never felt that I was a bad person. But I did not completely love myself then as I do now. Surgery made this possible by allowing me to feel settled in my skin and more of who I am.

I cannot remember how I found Professor Sava Perovic in Belgrade, Serbia, but I liked his metoidioplasty results. I was especially impressed that he was an urologist with a pediatric specialization in genetic anomalies rather than a cosmetic surgeon. He had an in depth understanding of male anatomy. He had also worked on men who suffered genital trauma and had progressed his practice to include sex reassignment surgery. At the time, information on the Professor was sparse in the U.S. He was very well known for his advancements in correcting urological pathologies and progressive thinking about gender, which was impressive. I read his publications and asked many questions. Having a medical background helped our conversations. He was gracious with his time, answering all my questions and emails. I felt an instant connection with him even though we were 7000 miles apart. I felt his compassion and sincerity to help men like me. He was a man of integrity and brilliance, who was constantly improving his work to give patients the best results possible. Money was not important to him. He was motivated to help people feel as good as possible in their bodies.

I decided to have metoidioplasty with the Professor, and, while I knew that intercourse might be difficult with a small penis, I was still excited to have one. I was excited by the chance to stand and pee and have sexual gratification like other natal men. Whether oral sex, manual stimulation, or my genitalia against hers, I was excited that my partner would be able to touch and feel my manhood. I also wanted the option of pursuing phalloplasty at a later time, and this procedure allowed that flexibility. I had a vaginectomy, scrotoplasty, and urethraplasty, which lengthened and rerouted my urethra, sutured my vagina, and implanted silicon testicles all in one surgery.

Preparations for the surgery meant getting in excellent physical shape. I dropped 40 pounds, even though I was already in good shape from working out regularly. I wasn't a smoker, and I ate a healthy diet. I took vitamin supplements to build up my immune system and to prepare my body, because I was worried about the travel time and jet lag.

The clinic staff was welcoming although their English was limited and my Serbian vocabulary was non-existent. They took excellent care of me the entire time, which was part of the deal for the agreed upon price with no additional hidden costs cropping up once in Belgrade. I liked that they only released me when they were certain that I was able to travel and did not pressure me to leave quickly. I stayed as long as I needed to heal.

My partner had the same concerns as any partner would of something of this magnitude, but she was supportive. She never pressured me to change my body. She just wanted me to be safe. Her main concern was that she could not go along to support me and could not be there during the surgery. Instead, I had a good friend come along to keep me company and help with getting back home. I did not tell my side of the family, but we did inform my partner's side of the family and they were supportive. I did not want to be stressed from dealing with all of my family's fears and was concerned that they would bombard my wife with questions, making her feel stressful also. I could not be their emotional support through this process when I needed support myself. I wanted to give my body the best chance of healing quickly and fully, which meant avoiding as much stress as possible.

I did not have any complications with surgery or healing. My doctors were surprised by how quickly I recovered. The most discomfort I felt was from my testicular implants. My balls were on fire! The pain was so intense that I visualized a little man sitting between my legs and scorching my nuts with a blowtorch. Just like any other guy, I had hoped that my phallus would have more length, but I was happy with its size. My pain management in the hospital was excellent, but after returning home, the sensitivity of my groin became obvious. I wore pants that were three sizes too large because of the swelling and need for room.

I did not anticipate the frequent need to urinate. I was sent home with both supra-pubic and Foley catheters. In the first couple of weeks of recovery, I voided through the supra-pubic tube, which was directly inserted into my bladder, rather than through the Foley catheter in my penis, which was still healing. When everything had healed and I was able to urinate from my penis, initially I had no control over where my stream went. Sometimes it shot out sideways or in a high arc. I had difficulty aiming directly into the toilet bowl. I did not anticipate the challenges of learning how to urinate all over again. I spent a lot of time cleaning up bathrooms. Peeing at night was a disaster. Often, I would be too tired to focus on the bowl and miss it much of the time. I eventually went back to sitting on the toilet at night. I just have to remember to point my penis down. Otherwise, my urine will arc outwardly. Occasionally, I sit to pee in public also.

My penis has a natural, normal look—more than I could have possibly imagined. The Professor positioned my implants so that one hung a little lower than the other, which is typical of natal male genitalia. I have received lots of compliments on my junk, but the biggest came from my own physician who was impressed with the aesthetics and functionality of my penis. He has since started referring other transmen patients to the Professor's practice.

In terms of sexual gratification I did not think sex could feel any better, but it does. It feels *so* much better. I have heightened sensation and am immensely more comfortable with my body during intercourse now. I now know what a blowjob feels like, and I understand why men lose their minds in enjoyment. My orgasms are more intense now. It is the most amazing thing I have ever experienced, short of penetrating a lover. Before surgery, sex was good and satisfying, but now, it is phenomenal. It overshadows everything I have ever done in the past. I like my erection and how it feels. The nerves that run up and down the shaft are so much more sensitive. My penis is more prominent, and having testicles and a scrotum now means that I have more area of sensitivity also. I like it when my partner plays with me now. Everything is outward and externalized. The stimulation is more pleasurable.

I like the natural ugliness of my penis. It is black and veiny and has a pink tip and looks just like an uncircumcised penis. It is not a waxy-looking shaft. Everything about it is natural and ugly, and this makes it the most beautiful thing on my body. I can now look at my body from head to toe and see and feel like the man I am. Now I see myself and think: *That is who I am. That's the man I'm supposed to be.*

For the first couple of months my wife and I just explored my body. We did not dive immediately into sex, because she did not know how to touch me. Not because she had not been with men, but because she was concerned about touching me too hard or too soft, and worried that she might interfere with my healing process. But eventually we figured things out. My partner gets more gratification from my body now. It's not that she did not enjoy it before, but rather it is that her pleasure has been enhanced now that I am able to enjoy my own body.

Although the surgery has changed me, my partner has also allowed me to be myself. Prior to surgery we always had an open and honest dialogue about what's going on with us and that's what this relationship has taught me: to be honest with myself and pursue surgery because it's what I need. I don't think I could have done this with any other partner without drama or struggling within myself. And she made it possible for me to move forward without added stress and struggle.

Talking with other men of color had a powerful impact on me. Many African American men do not see bottom surgery as a possibility for themselves. I certainly did not think that it was initially possible. But I am living proof that it is. I am sharing my journey because finding men of color to share our stories is difficult, and it is important to share my story with others to testify to our existence.

I am inspired to go to the next phase of MLD phalloplasty. Professor Perovic died in 2010, but I will be finishing the procedure with his protégé, Dr. Rados Djinovic. The funny thing is that I have to make some decisions about the size of my penis. My surgeons allow guys to choose the length and girth we want, and I am well aware of cultural notions that black men tend to have larger plumbing than men in other ethnic and racial groups. While I want to be reasonable, I also feel a need to represent. I want to please my partner sexually and size can matter in that department.

Transforming to Masculine Embodiment

Tone

When I first began considering bottom surgery I knew that phalloplasty was my ultimate goal. I decided to have a metoidioplasty first because I wanted to go through the stages of penile growth development like other cis-gender men. I had surgery on December 9ᵗʰ, 2010 with Dr. Miroslav Djordjevic and his fantastic team in Belgrade, Serbia. I knew that this route would be less costly. I wanted to give the testosterone time to work on my clitoris so that it would grow out as if it had been there since birth. I needed to feel like I was maturing from boyhood to manhood, and have time to adjust to all the physical and psychological changes of transitioning. In this way I am able to feel like I am growing into my manhood instead of changing my gender identity. I am planning to go for phalloplasty after I have finished school and lived through my adolescent phase. I also want to see how much more science and technology will develop in the next few years. I am only 24 and have faith that things will improve even more in the coming decade. For the time being my metoidioplasty penis allows me to feel less dysphoric and more centered in my body.

I am more than satisfied with the outcome of my surgery. Dr. Miro and his Belgrade team of surgeons are highly skilled. His main concern is achieving the best results for his patients. My worst moment in the hospital came immediately post-op when I found out that I had a hematoma. A hematoma is a very serious thing and can cause major problems if not handled immediately and properly. Dr. Miro aspirated the hematoma by pushing down on my pelvic region. It was a painful procedure and my screaming could be heard throughout much of the hospital. They had to take me back into the operating room to do it because it was too painful. But I am glad for their hands-on approach and attention to details like this, because it saved me from dealing with an even worst complication.

Going into surgery I had expected to have a fully functioning package, but I was surprised that they made my size a lot larger than I had expected. While I may not fall into the "average" range of natal male size, what matters is that I have my penis and testicles and they are fully functional. When I walk I can feel my penis and testicles, which gives me a feeling of relief and contentment. Statistically, two percent of the world's men have penises of less than four inches, which are about 130 million men. I have also enlarged my penis by using the Black Dragon Pump designed specifically for metoidioplasty penises and it has done wonders for me. The pump is similar to the one used by cis-gender men. I also used it before surgery, which helped my overall surgical results. Another enhancement method includes applying DHT (Dihydrotestosterone) directly to one's penis. Some men say that it enhances their size while others report little to no change. I did not use DHT because I did not want to take a chance on losing my dreadlocks.

Surgery did not make me a man. I have always been male. I was born male. Surgery was necessary because it allowed me to feel whole in my body and express myself as a man socially and sexually. It was too hard to look into the mirror and see how the lower half of my body contradicted my upper half. Testosterone was liberating me, changing my body and allowing me to be seen as the man I always knew myself to be. But I also felt stuck in an uncomfortable limbo that could jeopardize my safety at any moment depending on the situation. My body dysphoria also affected my relationships with women and cost me the love of my life, because I could not even talk about my feelings with her. I would not allow myself to be touched—not even hugged—and I just felt so out of place. It is miserable when you can't tell the person you love how badly you are feeling and suffering. I am choosing abstinence for the moment so I can focus on finishing school and transitioning with little distraction.

I don't feel ashamed of my body anymore or fear being naked in front of other people. My emotional connections with others are better now that I am not always clocking myself to make sure I'm passing as male. I feel much lighter and less burdened with that concern. I don't worry about being judged anymore, or of literally getting caught with my pants down. I feel safer a little safer in certain places. My gender presentation, identity and body all match now. Before surgery I couldn't get all my identification documents changed, which had a big impact on my life. This reduced my options for employment and where I could live because many places do background checks on applicants. It also held me back from going to college. But now I can apply for jobs and enroll in school without worry.

Going through transition and these surgeries in particular have brought me closer to my higher power. My higher power made me this way so that I could see the world differently from cis-gender men. I know the experiences and consciousness that I have as a man of trans experience would never have been possible if I had been raised male from birth. I can see and understand certain things from a woman's viewpoint. I think sometimes people might assume that transmen know what women think and feel, because we have lived in female bodies. Certainly there are many transmen who do understand what it's like to live at different points of the gender spectrum. But it shouldn't be assumed that all of us have a bi-gender consciousness. While I lived in a female body, I was also very male-identified and aligned my thinking more with men. Female socialization never imprinted on me. I rejected it at an early age. So I don't always see things like someone who may be woman-identified or bi-gendered.

When I began researching bottom surgery, I found little factual information and lots of rumors that stigmatized transmen who opt for it. This needs to stop because many men are hindered and hurt by misinformation about these surgeries. I have talked to surgeons and to men who have had bottom surgery. I have read surgical notes and medical journals, and I know the facts about bottom surgery. When talking about transition surgeries, we need to be more careful of our judgments and factual with information. One fiction of bottom surgery is that it is experimental and current procedures only mutilate people's genitals, leaving them worse off than before surgery. However, many transmen have sensate and aesthetically "passable" penises from both phalloplastic and metoidioplastic constructions. I also know men who can both penetrate and ejaculate after having metoidoplasty. It depends on the person's body and how the surgeon makes the urethral connection.

The cost of surgery and travel related expenses were my biggest concerns. I also had to consider the possibility of additional costs incurred from post-op complications and revisions. We have some highly skilled surgeons in the U.S., but I went to Serbia because it was much less expensive. As long as insurance companies continue rejecting trans surgeries as legitimate health care, people of trans-experience will continue going to other countries for surgery. My grandmother saw my determination after two years of struggling to save the money. Getting a good paying, full-time job was impossible because of the legal predicament with changing the gender marker on my identification documents. I was trying to save money by recycling aluminum cans and doing little odd jobs, but it was slow and seemed impossible. Every time I saved some money something bad happened and I had to use the money to cover it. I told my grandmother of my plans for surgery in 2010 but didn't ask her for money. I could never do that. It is my responsibility to take care of her now that I am grown and she is old. Later that day, she emailed me explaining that she had saved $10,000 in a CD for my college, which she wanted me to have for surgery. I was stunned and grateful! When I returned home from surgery, it meant the world to me to have her there. She was so supportive and has never once slipped and called me by anything other than my preferred name. She tells her friends to respect me as well. I love it.

I did not have problems with my family about transitioning. My folks just wanted me to be happy so I could succeed in life. I love and appreciate that my family takes the time to learn about what it means to have a transgender family member without my asking them. Even my siblings support me and call me their big brother. I was worried about this at first, but all they care about is that they have a big brother to love. My parents, especially my mother and grandmother, have always supported me. To hear my mama call me "son" after all we have been through means the world to me. Sometimes when I am having a bad day, she'll call and say, "I love you son," which will lighten my heart and whatever emotional burdens I am carrying. I also have two sons and they know and love me as their dad. I may not have much money but I have my family and that's the most important asset I can ever have.

Most people assume that because my family is Muslim and Southern Baptist with Jamaican roots, they would be in an uproar about my transition. They were not. They came to terms with who I am and never stopped loving me. My grandmother's religion teaches love and acceptance. She raised my father and uncles to accept and not hate and discriminate against people. Her love and her support have been so important in my transition. Some people assume that Muslims are shunned by our family and community when we transition, but this generalization is simply untrue for many Muslims of trans experiences. Anyone of Muslim faith who speaks against LGBT people is not following the teachings of Islam. Islam does not teach hate or intolerance of those who are different. In Creation there are no mistakes, only gifts to be received and lessons to be learned. Elders of some of the oldest Mosques in the world see nothing wrong with a man living comfortably as a woman and vice-versa, and transgender surgeries are performed in many Islamic countries.

My father has been on board about my transition from the first day, which has made it easy to talk to him about things. My mother does not have a drop of hate in her heart either. I am her child first and foremost—flesh and blood formed from her body. That's how she thinks of me. So she will always love me. Her father actually called me seconds before I boarded the plane to leave for Belgrade for surgery to check on me and make sure I was okay.

I went through three surgeries in seven months and the only comfort I had was a cellphone, email, and instant message communication from family and friends. For those of you who have partners, cherish them and be thankful. These surgeries are hard to endure alone. I had no one there for me when I awoke from surgery, but I knew I had a large support group back home. It's manageable solo, just not as easy when a loving person is there with you.

I learned from this experience that I am strong and determined to succeed and that I can achieve anything. I went through an emotional time in Belgrade, but it had nothing to do with the surgery itself. I was gaining clarity about some relationships in my life. I realized that I needed to cut some folks out of my life who weren't treating me well. People who swore they were my friends but never bothered to check on me in recovery. It was those whom I least expected who went out of their way to make sure that I was okay. I also cried too because I had just gone through the worst break-up in my life. After two years of thinking that crying was a display of weakness for a man, I finally just let it all out. It was so emotionally overwhelming at times to realize how far I had come and finally reached a point of wholeness and feeling good in my body. I feel like I have a new beginning and an opportunity to know myself in a new way. Every day feels like a wonderful blessing.

People react differently to my decisions about bottom surgery. I am surprised by how many friends, especially my lesbian friends, want to know if I've "gone all the way" (as they put it) in my transition. They ask all sorts of personal questions about my surgery like if my penis really works, what size it is and whether I am happier now as a man. A few have even asked to see my junk! I find their curiosity intriguing since I thought that lesbians weren't supposed to be interested in men or male genitalia. But I think people are curious about the genius of medical science.

Advice

Some words of advice about pre-op decisions. First, never settle for what others think is right for you. Trust your own feelings and instincts, because you have to live with the outcome. The woman I was partnered with while researching my surgical options was okay with my getting metoidioplasty, but she discouraged me from pursuing phalloplasty. She did not like the aesthetics or functioning, but I know now, after extensive research, that her opinion was based on myths and stigmas of phalloplasty. Because my clitoris was rather large, moreover, she felt that a metoidioplasty would be just fine. While I knew that metoidioplasty was a temporary stage in my transition to phalloplasty, I still found myself trying to appease her at the time. Sadly, she is no longer in my life, but luckily I kept my plans for phalloplasty. I have learned to trust my feelings and inner voice over the opinions of others.

Secondly, healing and recovery can be a bitch if you don't take care of yourself and treat your body right prior to surgery. If you stay in shape and eat healthy, your chances of healing and bouncing back faster will increase. Diet is important. Avoid junk food, soda, and trans fats. Eat balanced meals that include fiber, vegetables, whole grains, protein, and good carbs. Take vitamins to strengthen your immune system. Beyond watching my diet, I also had to prepare my body physically. I did a lot of core exercises for abs, oblique, and glutes, which helped get me through not only bottom surgery, but also through the hysterectomy as well. Muscles that are well toned before surgery regain their form quicker afterwards than flabby muscles.

If you smoke, *stop*! Smoking can jeopardize your recovery and healing, and you will probably have a hard time finding a surgeon to operate on you without requiring that you stop for surgery. I've seen some poor surgical re-sults on the bodies of smokers. It damages your cardiovascular system, which is vital for healing. It's not just the nicotine, but it's all the other bad chemi-cals in cigarettes that damage your body as well. It constricts the blood flow to veins and arteries, which is necessary for healing properly. If blood circulation is compromised, then all sorts of complications could occur, including skin graft failure, wound closure problems, and necrosis or tissue death. It could also affect how much sensation you regain in your penis. And finally, smoking diminishes your lung capacity, which does not bode well for people undergoing extended surgeries under anesthesia. So do yourself a favor and quit now.

Hanging On: Lou Sullivan's Embodiment of Gay Identity

Brice D. Smith

Lou Sullivan (1951-1991) is one of the most significant people in trans history because of the role he played in forging an international FTM community and in transforming understandings of the relationship between gender identity and sexual orientation. Lou dedicated his life to helping other trans people embody their identities. His activism stemmed from his own struggles to be a gay man in a time when gay FTMs supposedly did not exist, and Lou's quest for self-actualization resulted in gay FTMs receiving greater access to transition treatment. Of primary importance to Lou—and by extension, his activism—was undergoing bottom surgery, for it enabled him to embody and experience being a gay man in some of the most fundamental and intimate ways.[1]

As a child Lou was a shy, awkward girl[2] whose favorite pastime was "playing boys." In adolescence Lou translated "playing boys" into dressing like his favorite pop stars—first the Beatles and later Bob Dylan. He did not have many friends, and frequently escaped into all-male erotic fantasies. As a teenager Lou enjoyed the attention he received from boys, but had an inexplicable sense of disconnect from their attraction. At the age of 14, he wrote in his diary: "I don't want to be a girl. I hate it. I don't want it. Oh, sure. It makes me feel good when a boy looks at me and smiles. Or whistles. Sure.

But that's just because they like the way I look, not because they like me. I want that."[3]

In fall 1968, Lou began an 11-year relationship with Mark,[4] who was often read as gay due to his effeminate appearance and mannerisms. Shortly before meeting Mark, Lou had come to the self-realization that "male homosexuals REALLY turn me on," and he secretly hoped that Mark was gay.[5] During sex Lou imagined he and Mark were two gay men, and he encouraged Mark to pursue sexual relationships with other men largely so that Lou could vicariously live out his fantasy of being a gay man.

Three years into their relationship, Lou witnessed an intimate flirtatious exchange between Mark and another man that highlighted the inherent limitations of his female body in his sexual longings:

> No matter how I tried, I could never have joined their game. I felt a deep sadness at finally realizing I'll never have my deepest, secret dream fulfilled, ever. The guy lowered his eyelids & took Mark's hand as we left the car...I had an urge to lean over & kiss the boy as I left the car...but I knew I could never be part of the life & I had just admitted it to myself...I left the car hoping he didn't notice I was female...[6]

Lou envied Mark, who could go to a gay bar and come home any night of the week with a beautiful "youngman".[7]

> I wouldn't even be welcomed into the bar...and even if I got in, I'd be so ashamed that I was a woman that I'd leave quickly, lost, apologetically, and want to cry in desperation. I don't even know if there was anyone that's ever felt as I do...how they coped, what they did...how do I find out what someone like me does?[8]

One night, at the age of 21, Lou decided to revisit his childhood pastime of "playing boys" by wearing a leather jacket and pretending to be his idol, Lou Reed, in a local bar. For Lou, it was "one of the best times I've ever had!...I was the big stud guy." Writing about the experience in his diary the following day, it became apparent that Lou was no longer just playing: "For the first time in public, I was the man hiding inside of me for so many years.... But shit, I was real!!"[9] By cross-dressing, Lou could carry out his fantasy of being a gay man without having to live vicariously through Mark. He began going to gay bars in male leather drag on a regular basis, introducing himself as Lou, and saw himself as "2 people finally coming together in peace with each other."[10]

While cross-dressing and being read as male brought Lou a certain peace, he also experienced an "identity crisis."[11] Lou did not know how someone born female who felt male and desired gay men would identify. When he learned about transsexuals, Lou could relate to the idea of having "sex or gender role disorientation and indecision."[12] But at the time he was not particularly interested in so-called "corrective surgery," because "it seems the female-to-male change only involves a hysterectomy and/or a mastectomy... but no penis. What's the point?...[T]hat's what's Important, isn't it? That's what makes you a man."[13] So Lou began identifying as a female transvestite, despite the fact that the identity did not exist in either the medical literature on gender dysphoria or the popular imagination. By the end of his life Lou was credited with making *female transvestite* a viable identity category outside the medical establishment. Though his own identity would change over time, Lou continued to argue for the validity of female transvestite identity and its inclusion under the *FTM* category, which helped pave the way for the subsequent emergence of *transgender* as an umbrella term in the 1990s.

Identifying as a female transvestite gained Lou admittance into Milwaukee's gay bars and organizations. Lou went to gay bars multiple times a week where he flirted and danced with drag queens and gay men, and was occasionally successful at picking up men. But despite the joys of sleeping with gay men, at times Lou would become depressed and feel guilty, thinking "I have to make boys be heterosexual to have sex with them."[14] Still, he embraced his newfound freedom and acceptance into the "gay world." Emboldened by his experiences, Lou made his foray into trans activism by working as the contact person for information on transvestism in Gay Peoples Union and publishing several articles on transvestism in their *GPU News.*

Lou began warming up to the idea of transitioning in fall 1974. He wanted to be like "all these F-M TSs [FTM transsexuals] that have the mastectomy & the hormones but still have all their genitals in[tact] & still use them—still get off on the sensations, etc." But Lou also had reservations and "guilt feelings [that] I can't be half & half like that."[15] Mark was resistant to the idea of Lou's transitioning as well. Mark's acceptance of Lou's desire to be a gay man was confined to action and did not extend to embodiment. While he was supportive of Lou sleeping with gay men and being active in the gay community, Mark did not want Lou taking steps to physically transition and thus embody his desire to be a gay man.

In summer 1975, Lou and Mark moved to San Francisco. Lou confessed in his diary that he was "a little scared of the gay community in SF, that they won't accept me like I've been here [in Milwaukee] because I'm straight and female."[16] But he also yearned for change. San Francisco was quickly becoming a gay mecca, and—as a seemingly added bonus—the world-renowned Stanford University Gender Dysphoria Program was located in nearby Palo Alto.

Lou would later remember the next four years as "the most tormenting stage of my life."[17] He longed for community but felt that his embodiment foreclosed the possibility of membership in San Francisco's gay community. And though he now had far greater access to trans services, Lou eschewed transitioning for fear of losing Mark, who had become avowedly heterosexual. Lou eventually came to understand denying his desires to transition as denying his true being.

By mid-1979, Lou had severed his relationship with Mark and taken an active leadership role in the burgeoning trans community. Lou served as Treasurer for the Bay Area's Golden Gate Girls/Guys and edited their monthly *Gateway* newsletter. He also began fostering an international FTM communication network.

At the same time, Lou began mingling in San Francisco's gay scene. For a while, he enjoyed going cross-dressed to the bars and discos where he cruised and pretended to be like all the other guys there. But, unlike in his Milwaukee youth, Lou now avoided talking to the men for fear that they would discover he was female and ruin the illusion. His fears proved to be justified, for when Lou became bolder, the cruising transactions halted once cissexual (or non-transsexual) gay men "discovered" he was female. Lou became increasingly frustrated with being a female transvestite in San Francisco's gay world, and what he wanted more than anything else was to be a man.

In fall 1979, at age 28, Lou revisited the idea of transitioning. "Thinking hard & close about who I am," he wrote in his diary:

Just who I am and what I am, alone, and what I want for my-self.... In my need for a man in my bed, I detach myself from my body and my body becomes his; I stroke his hair, I see his wrist. I feel the warm winds blowing my open shirt from my smooth, hard flat chest. I catch the hungry eyes of another beautiful youngman. I reconsider male hormones—try to remember why I decided against them before. I could shave...I could take them!...I can see myself following my own dreams, regardless of ANYONE else's opinions.... It would all be worth the trouble.... I KNOW myself & who I am.[18]

Lou wanted to go through a "reputable clinic" like Stanford University's Gender Dysphoria Program to transition, but he had also heard that gender clinics would not touch him with "a 10-foot pole" because he identified as gay.[19] Lou sought the wisdom and support of FTM Steve Dain, who had transitioned in Stanford's program and was now working as a counselor at the National Sex Forum. It angered Dain that the (cissexual) medical professionals specializing in the diagnosis and treatment of transsexualism felt that transsexuals had to "fit a prescribed mold"—and a decidedly heteronormative one.[20] He confirmed that it was only Lou (rather than the so-called experts) who could know and decide his transsexual identity, and that he had a perfect right to be a gay man. Dain proved to be the guiding light that Lou needed: "I really needed for someone who knows to acknowledge the importance of the feelings I have had for so long.... I can see the pieces of my life falling into place and am extremely optimistic about my future."[21]

Lou applied to the Stanford clinic multiple times and was rejected. He was enraged by their ignorance and homophobia in rejecting him because of his sexual orientation. However, another development in the treatment protocol of transsexuals was also unfolding, which opened up the possibility of Lou pursuing sex reassignment outside the university-run gender clinics: the Harry Benjamin Standards of Care. When this treatment protocol was implemented, other avenues opened up for trans people to medically transition outside the university-run clinics. Lou was living in the midst of a "significant shift in the organization of transgender health care services" that transformed medico-scientific discourses of transsexuality and paved the way for gay FTMs like Lou to transition.[22] Through personal relationships and community contacts Lou was able to get a referral to an endocrinologist, regardless of his sexual orientation. "I keep thinking what a relief it will be to be in the gay men's world, finally, as a man," Lou wrote in his diary. "I'll still have a woman's body [without genital reconstruction]—but at least my outward appearance & my mind will be together—for the first time!"[23]

The most noticeable change in Lou during the first months of hormonal therapy was his relationship to his body and how he perceived himself. He now felt confident about participating in San Francisco's gay sexual subculture, as demonstrated one evening in January 1980. Lou began the evening at a gay porn theatre. He was hesitant about going in the backrooms, but took a seat in the theater where a man soon sat down next to him. As the two began fondling each other, Lou became nervous that his "sock-penis & balls might not pass" and tried to indicate through his actions that "I would do him but he couldn't do me." Eventually the man got up and left, but Lou was not discouraged. He headed for the drag bars and noticed how his perspectives had changed since beginning testosterone: "Instead of just watching the show & feeling self-conscious & worried I'd be read [as female], I was aware of who I liked & who was looking at me. Now when someone's looking, I think they're cruising me instead of reading me." Lou caught the eye of a drag queen and took her back to his place. Lou was initially embarrassed to disrobe, "but she was really free & open & told me not to be that way, that we are all okay no matter what we are." The drag queen made Lou feel relaxed and good about himself, and after they had had sex, she told Lou that he "was going to make a really great gay boy!"[24]

After four months of hormonal therapy Lou returned to the gay porn theatre and ventured into the backrooms. He was "surprised and truly delighted [by] the display of affections & feelings going on in these reputed dens of anonymous sex." He had not expected such encounters of tenderness to transpire among strangers engaging in public sex: "Somehow those brief displays of tenderness between two men mean more to me than I can say." Lou was also surprised to discover "how small all their cocks were," and realized that with metoidioplasty surgery and testicular implants, an FTM could "pass off as good as these guys did!"[25]

Metoidioplasty (or "freeing the clitoris," as the procedure was then called) was a new type of bottom surgery available to FTMs. The procedure was popularized by Stanford's Dr. Donald Laub, and was made possible by the masculinizing effects of testosterone on FTMs' genitals. Metoidioplasty provided FTMs with an alternative to phalloplasty which, as a procedure first used on veterans injured during World War I, operated under the notion of fulfilling an absence rather than building upon what was already there. Lou first learned about this new procedure from Dain, who had gotten a metoid-ioplasty with testicular implants from Laub at Stanford. When showing Lou the results of his bottom surgery, Dain also dissuaded Lou from feeling guilty about stimulating his vagina. Dain took the position that they could not help being born with the "female sexual apparatus & response," and that there was no reason for FTMs to deny themselves such sexual pleasure.[26]

The sexual pleasure Lou experienced in the backrooms was limited to administering oral sex. While doors to such gay sexual spaces were now open to Lou because of the physical effects of hormones, he remained fully clothed lest they be slammed shut. Lou assumed gay men would know nothing about transsexualism and was "scared to try to fool" them into believing that he was cissexual.[27] The confidence Lou experienced after beginning hormonal therapy quickly gave way to insecurities about his non-surgically-altered body. Lou came to believe that having a male chest would help him feel less awkward with gay men, and through his trans connections, Lou successfully pursued top surgery.

As Lou predicted, he felt more confident "being a man, sexually & so-cially" after top surgery.[28] He took a new job with an engineering company, and had several successful sexual liaisons with gay men in a short period of time, including a highway patrolman and a sailor. The sailor was aware of Lou's anatomy but never asked any questions and treated Lou just like any other gay man with whom he had spent the night. He asked Lou about the Club Baths, leading Lou to declare "this guy is a real life homosexual. No weekender." Lou watched him closely "trying to learn from him."[29] In October 1980, Lou published the first edition of *Information for the Female-to-Male Crossdresser and Transsexual*, which would serve for many years as the primary and most influential source of information on cross-dressing and transsexual-ism for countless FTMs. Included in the booklet were suggestions to FTMs on how to communicate with sexual partners about their trans embodiment. "Don't expect to hide your past from your lover," Lou advised. "It doesn't do any good to call the subject anything but what it is—sex change."[30] But at the same time, Lou found it difficult to communicate with sexual partners about his own body. In less than a month, he had three sexual interactions that left him feeling rejected, insecure, and anatomically inadequate. The first was with a Latino who kept warning Lou that "he's different, he's not human," to which Lou replied "that's good because I'm not human either, so we'll get along fine." When Lou stripped down to his jockey shorts, the man asked Lou if they were "different." Lou said "not that different," but the man quickly gathered up his things and left.[31] The second involved a white man who refused to honor Lou's wishes not to be touched, and Lou felt forced to inform him that he was "deformed" and "[had] no cock." The man told Lou that it was no big deal, that he needed to accept it, and that Lou should give people a chance. This angered and frustrated Lou, who felt like the man would think differently if he were in Lou's position.[32] The third incident involved a black man. "All fine until he discovered I had no cock," according to Lou. "[He] claimed it made no difference, [but then] he couldn't get a hard-on thereafter & kept asking 'What ARE you?!!!' though I explained in minute detail over & over. Then he remembered he had to leave."[33]

Hormones and top surgery had enabled Lou to feel like he was accepted unequivocally as a gay man—socially. But Lou felt like he was in no-man's land sexually and, for Lou and others, sex was the primary means of validating one's gay identity. Lou found it difficult to "allow myself the pleasure of finally being one of my group, finally join the class of gay men, letting myself fit in the way I feel I do" without reconstructing his genitals.[34] When Lou looked in the mirror, he could "hardly believe how beautiful" he was. "I feel so desirable, yet I can't offer myself to a partner," he wrote. "If I had a man's genitals I could be so much freer with potential lovers".[35]

> It seems so foreign to me when I see how freely & openly everyone around me is with their bodies. I realize that I don't even give potential lovers a second glance, or encourage even the slightest any men who are attracted to me. And I know they are. I am beautiful! It hurts me too much to encourage them, or to even notice their attentions to me. I can't stand to see someone offering themselves to me, and my having to deal with this fucking body. It's just not fair.... I am a good person & deserve something better than this.... I want to sleep with a man. I want to wrap myself around him. I want to offer myself unconditionally & unapologetically. I should be free to feel all the warmth & love I do.[36]

In summer 1981, Lou met a 20-year-old "gorgeous boy" named Keith and immediately fell in love. Lou's initial impression of Keith led him to think: "It's supposed to work. One day I'll find someone who likes me so much [that being trans] won't matter."[37] Believing Keith to be that person, Lou told Keith that he was transsexual. In terms of friendship this news did not matter to Keith. But as their relationship intensified and became increasingly physical, Keith, who identified as straight, struggled to understand his attraction to Lou and, by extension, his (sexual) identity given Lou's trans embodiment: "[Keith] said, 'But I don't even know what you are!' I said 'yes you do, I've been very honest with you.'" Lou explained: "What I want is to be able to function as a gay man. But I can't. So I do whatever I can.... He said 'But what ARE you? You're not a man & you're not a woman!' I said 'Well I guess I'm just ME then.'" Then Keith asked Lou to take off his clothes: "I didn't feel self-conscious. I just stripped myself & thought: this is it, and I love you so goddamned much I'm laying myself at your feet. I can't be hurt. You can't hurt me, because I believe you love me too.... I stood in front of him naked & heard him mutter '...beautiful.'"[38] Lou was "overwhelmed how good sex is with someone I love so much."[39] He also marveled at how, "I am there when I have sex with [Keith]":

> I am not fantasizing about men together, or of some other sex scene—I am feeling my body against his—I am feeling his hands touching me—I am excited as I look at him as he looks at me. Such feelings I've never known. He always refers to me in the masculine & there is no doubt we are two men who love each other.[40]

Keith moved in with Lou and they lived together for the next five years. Before transitioning Lou had been saddened at the thought "that if I got together with a gay man, I would have to turn him heterosexual in order to have a relationship with me." But Lou felt "so proud, and isn't it wonderful, that Keith had to turn homosexual in order to have a relationship with me! That he had to present himself as a gay man to our friends and neighbors. Just for that fact, my whole sex change was worth it!"[41] Though others identified Keith as a gay man by virtue of his relationship with Lou, he personally came to identify as bisexual.

Initially, Lou's relationship with Keith allowed Lou "to admit/learn/accept/enjoy" his female genitals "very much."[42] Lou remembered what Dain had said about a lot of other FTMs using their "holes" too: that they were afraid that admitting it would render their manliness questionable.[43] This was no concern for Lou because he felt like Keith saw and treated him like a man: "[He] always speaks of me with masculine pronouns, even 'his pussy'," which Lou found amusing.[44] But over time, the lack of variation in their sexual repertoire changed Lou's perspective. Lou wanted to penetrate Keith during sex, and worried that he would never know what it was like to be a man unless he could penetrate someone. His sense of being anatomically inadequate reared up again and translated into a more general sense of being inadequate as a man:

> I can never be a man until my body is whole and I can use it freely and without shame. I may appear in all outward ways to be a man and I may feel in my heart all that a man feels, yet my spirit is hampered and my dreams of being a whole man will always be just dreams.... I cannot even fool myself when I stand face-to-face with another man and he is full of pride & privilege & confidence that has been his birthright.[45]

When Lou's father died in fall 1983, he inherited enough money to make genital surgery a financial possibility. Over the next year, Lou worried about how bottom surgery might affect his relationship with Keith, who resisted anything but vaginal penetration. But at the same time Lou did not want to lose himself, as he had with Mark, and he also became sexually frustrated by having what he called "girlsex."[46] Lou never doubted Keith's love for him, but he doubted that Keith loved him as a man. Keith insisted that he saw and loved Lou as a man, but Lou felt that Keith was only attracted to his female genitals and thus did not see or desire him as a man. Further blurring the relationship was the fact that Keith began a serious relationship with a cissexual woman. By the end of 1984 Lou had once again come to despise his body.

While Lou had found an endocrinologist and surgeon for top surgery with ease, he found it tremendously difficult finding a surgeon for bottom surgery outside of the university-run gender clinics. It took 18 months for Lou to locate a surgeon. Most of the surgeons who performed FTM bottom surgeries were affiliated with programs that continued to reject gay FTMs. One notable exception was Dr. Stanley Biber whose practice in Trinidad, Colorado, was one alternative, but he only performed phalloplasty surgery, not the metoidioplasty surgery that Lou wanted. Lou's seemingly endless quest for genital reconstructive surgery made him feel "so goddamned tired of being a freak," and like "Life is passing me by and everyone else finds their slot, but I'm always on the outside looking in."[47] But then Lou discovered that "good ole Dr. [Michael] Brownstein" had recently performed his first metoidioplasty with testicular implants on an FTM whom Lou knew. Brownstein had done some surgical revisions of Lou's chest in fall 1984, and continues to specialize in top surgeries to this day. Lou was ecstatic in anticipation of genital surgery:

> It's like before it would never happen, and now suddenly it's happening NOW. I suddenly feel ALIVE and awakened to myself, imagining I have a cock and balls! [A]nd how will I be different?? I feel cocky, and what an appropriate word with my true feelings all in one.... How much more OUT FRONT must men feel, how much better able to feel proud of their bodies, since they have everything displayed.... It's going to be such an exciting existence just having an intact body like everyone else and I can stop feeling ashamed and unworthy and gross.[48]

Lou was excited about the prospect of finally being a "real man."[49] Three days before surgery, Lou reflected:

> I feel very positive and not like I'm changing my body at all, but like I'm finally going to have something permanent between my legs and will have some sex organs!...I am finally finishing what I began 6 years ago. It's about time. Because I look at what I have now and I don't SEE it, like when I never saw my face in the mirror before hormones and suddenly my face appeared, the voice I heard coming out of my mouth was finally mine. I so look forward to looking between my legs and seeing my sex.[50]

On 22 April 1986, Lou underwent metoidioplastic reconstruction with urethral extension and testicular implants with Brownstein. Lou did not feel so much like a different person, but rather that he was "free from a mental prison."[51] He felt sexy after his surgery and looked forward to being able to masturbate and to beginning an avid sex life that summer. But Lou began experiencing post-surgical complications almost immediately. Less than two weeks after undergoing surgery, Lou's left testicular implant burst: "I was ready to ride that big wave of loving my body and wanting others to love it, and to loving and wanting theirs. But the humiliation of my incomplete body continues to plague me." When Brownstein removed the implant, Lou "felt like I'd been amputated." Lou mourned the loss, but Brownstein was optimistic. Eventually Lou "[felt] pretty macho and butch, having endured this pain. Really proves how much I want this, how much better I feel as a man."[52]

Two months after Lou's initial surgery, Brownstein tried to reinsert Lou's left testicular implant, but complications developed again and resulted in its removal a second time. Lou would have to wait at least six months before trying to have his implant inserted again: "Of course I feel sorry for myself. But I am happy I have something."[53] While healing, Lou contemplated his relationship with his body and with others:

> I'm really feeling I need to fall in love with myself before involving myself in another intimate relationship. That was why I wanted to change my sex in the first place...so that I could love myself, sleep with myself, know myself and enjoy everyday living. It's as though I'm playing my favorite game all day, and now it's just become so easy and natural and fun that I don't want anything else. I want to learn to love my body and feel all its sensations, to be with other guys who look at my body and they want to "dick off" too. It sure is hard when my body won't cooperate with my quickly changing psyche.[54]

Activism was a good distraction for Lou from his bodily struggles. For several years he had been communicating with FTMs around the world, and he began working with FTMs in the Bay Area to start an FTM group.

> I'm very excited by the idea of calling a gathering of F ®M's just to talk to each other, exchange information, and just "be there" for new F ®M's coming out, and in steering them away from [the Stanford University Gender Dysphoria Program], and toward Brownstein, who

I really talked up. I'm very excited…oh, I already said that…but I am, about maybe even getting a small newsletter going and I'm sure it's possible if we can get other F ®M's to "sign up." And you know how I LOVE to put little newsletters together![55]

The first FTM "Get-Together" was held on 6 December 1986. Over the years the organization would become FTM International, and Lou's *FTM* newsletter became a lifeline to thousands of FTMs and their significant others around the world.

As 1986 drew to a close, Lou's life was filled with new beginnings. In addition to starting the FTM organization and its newsletter, Lou and Keith parted ways amicably and he was scheduled for surgery with Brownstein on January 13, 1987. But then the seemingly unthinkable happened: on New Year's Eve Lou was diagnosed with AIDS.

Such news put Lou in "a state of shock and disbelief." For one thing, AIDS was associated with promiscuity while Lou considered himself as having been "a sexual recluse for so long."[56] He would later tell renowned "gender professional" Dr. Ira Pauly: "I would've loved to be promiscuous. I admire and I think it must be wonderful to feel that good about your body and that free to be running around and having sex all the time. I've never felt that good about my body. Ever."[57] Lou was also stunned because he had never considered the epidemic an immediate threat to him. Despite identifying as a gay man, Lou still harbored self-doubts as to whether or not he *was* a gay man, and AIDS had been portrayed as a decidedly gay disease. It was this way of thinking that led Lou to write, in the first diary entry after receiving his AIDS diagnosis:

> …[I]nside I feel serene and a certain kind of peace. My whole life I've wanted to be a gay man and it's kind of an honor to die from the gay men's disease. I'm going to take special pleasure in informing [those at the former Stanford University Gender Dysphoria Program]—I'll write something like: "Your clinic decided that I couldn't live as a gay man, but I am going to die like one."[58]

Though it was genital reconstructive surgery that enabled Lou to feel like he fully embodied his gay identity, for the broader public in the mid-1980s, AIDS had become the embodiment of gay identity. In his correspondence, publications in the gay and trans presses, lectures, interviews, conversations with other FTMs—any time he spoke about his identity after being diagnosed with AIDS—Lou repeated derivations of this line that he initially shared with the gender professionals from Stanford.

One of Lou's biggest concerns upon receiving his AIDS diagnosis was that it might "prevent me from ever completing my surgery." He immediately contacted Brownstein, who "was very upset and said he felt awful."[59] When Lou told Brownstein that he did not think any surgeon would operate on him because of AIDS, Brownstein said that HIV status should not prevent someone from embodying their identity. Despite the potential risks, Brownstein knew how much the surgery meant to Lou, and he wanted to finish what he started for this "special guy."[60] Two months later Brownstein reinserted Lou's left testicular implant without any complications.

Lou struggled with the cruel irony of contracting AIDS at such a pivotal moment in his life. "The thing that hurts me most," he wrote after speaking with Brownstein in early January, "is to think that I will never know a man's loving touch on my whole complete body":

> That even though I may still be able to undergo the surgery to get my left testicle, that because of my disease I will never find a lover who will suck me, lick me, kiss me there. The enormous injustice of that possibility almost overwhelms me with despair. How close I was! How good it feels to have even one ball! [A] miniscule cock! And now I feel like a leper, something diseased and fearsome and unlovable. This is what is haunting me. Not the imminence of death. We all know from the moment we are born that we are destined to die. That's OK. I just dread having to spend these last precious years as an outcast AGAIN.[61]

Lou redoubled his activism after being diagnosed with AIDS, more determined than ever to use his experiences to help others. His work included educating members of the trans community about their susceptibility to contracting the disease. As demonstrated in a lecture he gave to FTMs, Lou was very perceptive of how some trans people's genital situations might make them vulnerable to taking certain sexual risks:

I think the TS [transsexual] community is at very high risk for AIDS for a number of reasons, particularly because we all know how hard it is to get sex partners. We have special circumstances with our bodies, then go through a tense courtship after finally attracting someone, and you don't want to throw any obstacles in the way. If someone is going to be nice to us, touch us and love us, we don't want to say "no." We're so desperate for physical contact that we throw caution to the wind and say to ourselves, "Well, it's just this one time…it'll be OK…."

I think we're at a mental disadvantage because we have such problems with our bodies in the first place. Our bodies aren't something we want to care for or nurture. We've struggled with our bodies, they don't function for us correctly, the surgeries are lousy…we live our lives with a negative body image which prevents us from taking care of ourselves because we're so busy adjusting ourselves. It's a self-esteem problem.

Lou also believed that some FTMs and MTFs experience "psychological barriers" with using safer sex items like dental dams and condoms, because they were designed for use by non-trans bodies and did not take "our individual unique body statuses" into consideration. He concluded his lecture by using the desire for sex reassignment as motivation for FTMs to be aware of HIV/AIDS transmission and to practice safer sex: "[T]hink about your surgery, because if you're going to get sick, you're not going to be strong enough to undergo any surgery, and you'll have a hard time finding a surgeon who'll deal with you. So keep yourself healthy so you can enjoy your change."[62]

In the years after his AIDS diagnosis, Lou became a world-renowned FTM activist and scholar. The greatest struggle he faced was the same one that had plagued him for his entire life: his relationship with his body and specifically in sexual relations with other men. Lou had long thought that genital surgery would allow him to fully embody his gay identity, primarily because of how differently he would experience his body while having sex. But at times, his AIDS diagnosis made Lou feel "that I was never meant to experience the ease with which people all around me use their bodies".[63]

I guess I just feel that my body has been one big burden throughout my life, and getting this fatal disease…one that can be transmitted to anyone who loves my body…is just the last straw. Just knowing that this is the way I will be until I die is so hard to accept. I haven't been a very fortunate person in this life…. I hate to think that my dream of being a man-loving man is doomed, especially now at this very moment when I've finally completed my surgery and am supposed to be adjusting to my new life and body.[64]

It took Lou about three months to adjust to his body after bottom surgery, when he was finally able to conclude that "It doesn't matter HOW I got the body I have, it only matters that I DO have the body I have."[65]

One summer evening, eight months after being diagnosed with AIDS, Lou sat in a Castro bar surrounded by "young lean smiling boys" and pondered his future:

I've come all this way, gone thru this whole change…Now what? My future compressed into a shortened time slot. Most [are] dead in 2 years. Some live for 5. What have I been striving toward?… Oh! to be "NORMAL." To be a mere victim of my lust, instead of having orchestrated my desires, my place here…. Yet it's been worth all the years just to be in this bar, here, now, with AIDS, and to be a man among men. Not to have to wonder if they think I'm a female… that I know is no longer an issue. To be included, however voyeuristically, however theoretically, in the society of men who can only openly proclaim their ardor for other men—as those within this bar—I have gladly endured these years and these trials. It may be "the love that dare not speak its name" but it is surely the love that endures, that persists against all condemnation, even through the threat of death, of AIDS, a love that cannot die; to me, this is the only REAL love.[66]

Avenues to gay male spaces suddenly opened up for Lou after surgery, and he was determined to enjoy his body as much as possible for the remainder of his time. He was upfront with sexual partners about having AIDS, but interestingly he chose not to disclose his trans history. Lou found the majority of his sexual partners through a club called Small Guys and Fans for men "hung like hamsters" and those who found small penises attractive.[67] In his personal ad for the club, Lou said that he had a "[one-inch] micropenis," and included "safe [sex] only. PWA OK."[68] He also went to gay jack-off clubs, which had become "very popular since AIDS," replacing a lot of the bath-houses and backrooms, and attended "nudie parties."[69] Having a penis allowed Lou to relax and enjoy the social dynamics of gay cruising and male energy, which was impossible before surgery when he worried about being discovered:

> Somehow I felt very relaxed and confident about going to this event—possibly all the weekly nude massages I've been getting has helped me feel relaxed about stripping down, and I guess my experiences at similar events have taught me that my body is pretty average compared to the other men there.... Of course my dick looks much different than everyone else's, but I figure all dicks look different and I'm confident no one will be mean to me there because I've got a small dick. I also realize that, as out of shape and pathetic as my body is, it will only get more out of shape and pathetic as days go by, and I probably look better today than I ever will, so I better seize the moment.... I am very proud of myself for feeling so confident about my status as a man and my realistic body image.[70]

Bottom surgery enabled Lou to feel confidently male and brought him the sense of belonging that he had always sought: to be a man among men. He felt this sense of belonging most deeply when attending a men's retreat. Initially, Lou was amazed at how comfortable and at ease he felt in a group of strangers, remembering how withdrawn he had been most of his life. Now, he attributed his newfound comfort to being accepted as a man:

> There was lots of intense and intoxicating male energy, and I became quite overwhelmed (one of the few times) and I just let the tears fall, thinking of my life, of the journey I've made, how sad and hopeless I was as a young person feeling I could never belong, never be one of the guys. And here I am, after so many years, so many struggles, here I am, a man among men, and not too bad of a one, either. I've found my place in this world, when before I felt so alienated, a creature from outer space. This "male bonding ritual" just seemed to bring me to the peak of my journey. I've made it! And then the irony, the brick wall,

the downward spiral of this disease in my body. But I feel so proud to have really reached my male aspirations, my goals, that to be faced with an end to my life seems not so awful.[71]

Lou's life came to end on March 2, 1991 three months shy of his 40th birthday. Reflecting upon his life, Lou wrote: "I feel like someone who's done something important and worthwhile with his life and I hold my head high," and that, "I have never regretted changing my sex, even for a second, despite my AIDS diagnosis, and in some twisted way feel that my condition is proof that I really attained my goal of being a gay man—even to the finish, I am with my gay brothers."[72]

Endnotes

1   With the exception of certain ellipses, and unless otherwise noted by the use of brackets, all quoted materials in this work appear as they do within Lou Sullivan's original documents. This includes his use of capitalization, underlining, bolding, and punctuation.

2   *Girl* has not been placed within quotation marks because Lou never denied his female past and critiqued the notion that he was (always) a male simply "born in the wrong body."

3   Louis G. Sullivan Diary [hereafter cited as Diary], 7 January 1987, box 1 folder 14, Louis Graydon Sullivan Papers, 91-7, the Gay, Lesbian, Bisexual, Transgender Historical Society [hereafter cited as LGS Papers].

4   Lou's lovers have been given pseudonyms in this chapter.

5   Diary, 2 May 1968, box 1 folder 8, LGS Papers.

6   Diary, 23 December 1972, box 1 folder 10, LGS Papers.

7   Lou borrowed the term *youngman* from author John Rechy whose novel *City of Night* had a profound impact on him.

8   Diary, 13 February 1973, box 1 folder 10, LGS Papers.

9   Diary, 26 February 1973, box 1 folder 10, LGS Papers.

10   Diary, 28 February 1973, box 1 folder 10, LGS Papers.

11   Diary, 12 April 1973, box 1 folder 10, LGS Papers.

12   Harry Benjamin, *The Transsexual Phenomenon* (New York: Warner, 1966), 31.

13   Diary, 31 May 1973, box 1 folder 10, LGS Papers.

14   Diary, 30 October 1973, box 1 folder 10, LGS Papers.

15 Diary, 1 November 1974, box 1 folder 10, LGS Papers.

16 Diary, 9 May 1975, box 1 folder 11, LGS Papers.

17 Lou, "FTM Male Box," *FTM* 15 (April 1991) in *FTM Newsletter, 1987-1992*, ed. Martin Rawlings-Fein (San Francisco: FTM International, Inc., 2005), 90.

18 Diary, 11 September 1979, box 1 folder 11, LGS Papers.

19 *Ibid.*

20 Diary, 28 September 1979, box 1 folder 11, LGS Papers.

21 Diary, 30 September 1979, box 1 folder 11, LGS Papers.

22 Susan Stryker, "Portrait of a Transfag Drag Hag as a Young Man: The Activist Career of Louis G. Sullivan," in *Reclaiming Genders: Transsexual Grammars at the Fin de Siècle,* ed. Kate More and Stephen Whittle (London: Cassell, 1999), 68.

23 Diary, 27 September 1979, box 1 folder 11, LGS Papers.

24 Diary, 14 January 1980, box 1 folder 12, LGS Papers.

25 Diary, 19 May 1980, box 1 folder 12, LGS Papers.

26 Diary, 17 February 1980, box 1 folder 12, LGS Papers.

27 Diary, 1 March 1980, box 1 folder 12, LGS Papers.

28 Diary, 12 March 1980, box 1 folder 12, LGS Papers.

29 Diary, 31 August 1980, box 1 folder 12, LGS Papers.

30 Louis Sullivan, *Information for the Female-to-Male Crossdresser and Transsexual*, 2d ed (San Francisco: Zamot Graphic Productions, 1986), 40-41.

31 Diary, 20 October 1980, box 1 folder 12, LGS Papers.

32 Diary, 10 November 1980, box 1 folder 12, LGS Papers.

33 Diary, 18 November 1980, box 1 folder 12, LGS Papers.

34 Diary, 10 February 1981, box 1 folder 12, LGS Papers.

35 Diary, 23 March 1981, box 1 folder 12, LGS Papers.

36 Diary, 25 June 1981, box 1 folder 12, LGS Papers.

37 Diary, 26 June 1981, box 1 folder 12, LGS Papers.

38 Diary, 22 August 1981, box 1 folder 12, LGS Papers.

39 Diary, 27 August 1981, box 1 folder 12, LGS Papers.

40 Diary, 1 October 1981, box 1 folder 13, LGS Papers.

41 Diary, 27 July 1987, box 1 folder 15, LGS Papers.

42 Diary, 5 November 1981, box 1 folder 13, LGS Papers.

43 Diary, 11 December 1981, box 1 folder 13, LGS Papers.

44 Diary, 24 November 1981, box 1 folder 13, LGS Papers.

45 Diary, 5 April 1983, box 1 folder 13, LGS Papers.

46   Diary, 14 September 1984, 26 September 1984, box 1 folder 13, LGS Papers.

47   Diary, 25 February 1986, box 1 folder 14, LGS Papers.

48   Diary, 13 April 1986, box 1 folder 14, LGS Papers.

49   Michael L. Brownstein, interview by author, 31 March 2007, Milwaukee; Diary, 13 April 1986, 19 April 1986, box 1 folder 14, LGS Papers.

50   Diary, 19 April 1986, box 1 folder 14, LGS Papers.

51   Diary, 24 April 1986, box 1 folder 14, LGS Papers.

52   Diary, 5 May 1986, box 1 folder 14, LGS Papers.

53   Diary, 15 July 1986, box 1 folder 14, LGS Papers.

54   Diary, 5 July 1986, box 1 folder 14, LGS Papers.

55   Diary, 4 October 1986, box 1 folder 14, LGS Papers.

56   Diary, 7 January 1987, box 1 folder 14, LGS Papers.

57   Ira Pauly, *Female to Gay Male Transsexualism: II—Living with AIDS* (Reno: Department of Psychiatry & Behavioral Sciences, University of Nevada School of Medicine, 1988).

58   Diary, 7 January 1987, box 1 folder 14, LGS Papers.

59   Diary, 7 January 1987, box 1 folder 14, LGS Papers.

60   Michael L. Brownstein interview.

61   Diary, 11 January 1987, box 1 folder 14, LGS Papers.

62   "Spring Get-Together Focuses on FTMs and AIDS," *FTM* 12 (June 1990) in *FTM Newsletter, 1987-1992,* ed. Martin Rawlings-Fein (San Francisco: FTM International, Inc., 2005), 65, 67.

63   Diary, 1 March 1987, box 1 folder 15, LGS Papers.

64   Diary, 10 April 1987, box 1 folder 15, LGS Papers.

65   Diary, 11 July 1987, box 1 folder 15, LGS Papers.

61   Diary, 15 August 1987, box 1 folder 15, LGS Papers.

67   Diary, 1 March 1987, box 1 folder 15, LGS Papers; Ron to [Lou Sullivan], undated, box 4 folder 172, LGS Papers.

68   Small Guys & Fans, 1 September 1987, box 4, folder 172, LGS Papers.

69   Diary, 1 March 1987, box 1 folder 15, LGS Papers; Ira B. Pauly, *Female to Gay Male Transsexualism: Part III* (Reno: Department of Psychiatry & Behavioral Sciences, University of Nevada School of Medicine, [1989]).

70   Diary, 15 October 1989, box 1 folder 15, LGS Papers.

71   Diary, 27 May 1989, box 1 folder 15, LGS Papers.

72   Diary, 27 September 1990, box 1 folder 16, LGS Papers, and Louis G. Sullivan to Ray Blanchard, 1 September 1987, box 2 folder 85, LGS Papers.

Phalloplasty

Michael Dillon is the first transsexual man known thus far to have a surgically constructed penis. He began phalloplasty in 1946 and completed the process in 1949 with Dr. Harold Gillies, who had invented the procedure to repair the genitals of war veterans. Dillon endured many lengthy surgeries and complications with healing. An excerpt from Pagan Kennedy's biography of Dillon (*The First Man-Made Man: The Story of Two Sex Changes, One Love Affair, and a Twentieth-Century Medical Revolution*) describing his surgical experience is included in this section.

Gillies invented the abdominal technique (sometimes called the "suitcase handle"), which harvests tissue (nerves, skin, adipose tissue, and blood vessels) from the lower abdominal region along the pelvic line. Initially, the doctor forms the penis in the shape of a suitcase handle along the pelvic line. A series of surgical delays are then performed to move and suture the penis mons pubis. This incremental approach preserves blood flow, reduces the possibility of necrosis, and minimizes other complications. The abdominal method is still used widely today by surgeons who have improved the technique, but the surgical field of genitoplasty has also expanded with the invention of other approaches.

Three additional surgical techniques have been developed that involve using tissue from the forearm, leg, and back. These are free-flap procedures. Instead of a gradual migration of tissue to the mons pubis in several surgical stages, these surgeries sever the donor tissue from its origins and transplant it to the groin in the initial stage. Nerves, skin, fatty tissue, blood vessels, arteries, and sometimes muscle are harvested from the donor region through a very delicate and lengthy microsurgical process, which enhances the possibility of sensation returning both inside and on the surface of the penis. The musculocutaneous latissimus dorsis (MLD) procedure additionally transplants a portion of the latissimus muscle from the back to enhance sensation and provide more girth and penile durability.

The technology for penile erection has also improved. Bendable silicon rods implanted in the penile shaft are one option, but reports of rods poking through men's penises during intercourse spurred a search for alternatives. The inflatable erectile prosthetic is another choice and has made advancements in the last few years. It is a three-part system composed of a reservoir of saline fluid implanted in the abdominal region, a pump placed in the scrotal sack, and one (or two) cylinders positioned in the penile shaft. Most surgeons anchor the cylinders to the pelvic bone to secure the system and prevent the kind of protrusion seen with the rods. To get an erection the pump is squeezed, pushing fluid from the reservoir into the cylinders and stiffening the penis. The most recent improvement of the pump includes cylinders that not only pump the penis into an erect position, but also expand outwardly to increase girth. This is an encouraging development because it means that less tissue is needed from the donor site to construct the penis. In turn, this means smaller surgical incisions, faster healing with fewer complications, less scarring, and improved aesthetics.

Trans men also invent their own erection technologies. Several contributors in this collection have developed clever techniques for achieving erections for intercourse. One technique involves layering the penis with two or more condoms. Another makes use of condoms and surgical wrapping gauze.

Other surgical procedures typically performed with phalloplasty are hysterectomy, oophorectomy, vaginectomy, scrotoplasty, urethraplasty, and prosthetic implantation. The latter three procedures are optional. This is not the case for hysterectomy, oophorectomy, and vaginectomy, which (to my knowledge) is mandatory in phalloplasties with urethral extensions and prosthetic implants. I am unaware of any surgeon who does this kind of phalloplastic construction without requiring these surgeries. And this is due to the architecture of both human anatomy and the three-part erectile prosthetic system. Sufficient space in the abdominal cavity must be available to implant the reservoir of saline. The uterus is removed to make room for the reservoir. An attempt to implant the reservoir alongside the uterus and ovaries would overcrowd the abdominal region, leading to severe pain and health complications, and likely sabotage surgical outcomes.

One Man's Junk

Declan

Even as a young child, I knew my penis was missing. It was distressing, sensing I should have something there on my body, yet I could not see or touch it, like a phantom limb of sorts. It was distressing enough that I had attempted to fill the empty space by placing various items into my underwear—rocks, socks, plastic bottles. And I was equally distressed over the genitals I did have. I knew they were wrong.

There are many terms for transgender folk. I consider myself to be a transsexual in the transgender world. From my earliest memories I knew I was a boy—not a little of this and a little of that, but plain and simple, I was a boy.

Transitioning was scary—there were so many aspects to tackle. But I was thrilled, to finally have an answer to what I suffered from, a name for it, and even more excited that things could be changed. There were surgeries and legalities that would allow me to live my life as the male I knew I was.

During my research of hormones, legal hoops, and surgeries, I'd continuously come across comments and information on how phalloplasty for transmen left something to be desired. Descriptions such as "mangled flesh," "frankendick," and "they fall off" were frequent. Most of these comments came from fellow transmen. And then of course the hefty financial cost needed to be considered to obtain one of these "frankendicks". Hence, early on in transition, I'd pretty much tossed the idea of bottom surgery to the side. It was heartbreaking and difficult to accept that I'd remain penis-less.

Everything along the road to transition was scary yet wonderfully exciting as well. But each step was cumbersome. The first thing I did was have top surgery—removal of the breast tissue and reconstruction for a male-appearing chest. When I woke up post-op, even through all the bandages and pain, I could feel that my chest was flat, the way it had felt in my head all along. That was 12 years ago, and I still wake up thankful for this comfort every day.

I then found an endocrinologist who treated transmen with testosterone. Initially I found friends to do the intramuscular injections for me until I became brave enough to do them myself. The effects of testosterone were bliss. My body gradually took on the shape I had envisioned: shoulders, back, and chest broadened, hips and butt narrowed. I was gaining the male upside-down triangle physique, which I knew was mine.

The entire legal name, gender, and birth certificate change process was daunting and exhausting. I hired a lawyer to submit the change to the courts, which went smoothly. With that I began the arduous task of changing the records of my entire life, which seemed to never end, but finally did.

I was living my life fully as a male and finally comfortable, except for one nagging item: my penis. It turned out I wasn't as okay without a penis as I thought I'd be. I still felt that haunting phantom organ. I still did not feel truly complete. And I remained distressed by the female genitals I did have. It was time to seriously seek bottom surgery.

Guys were starting to talk more about a surgery called metoidioplasty, where the clitoris is released or freed up. With this procedure, one could have what appeared to be a mini-penis, with optional scrotum and testicular implants. This was said by many people to be a safer option, as well as less costly. It gave me brief hope. But as I continued to look over photos of the results, I knew it wasn't going to help me. My mind said I had a reasonable-sized penis. I could feel the weight of it and the warmth of it as it lay against my thigh. The metoidioplasty looked just as surgeons themselves were describing it—like "a micro-penis" or "infantile genitalia." To me, it still looked a bit like female genitalia, but modified. It had no weight, it would not fill up my empty underwear, and it was not going to rest warmly against my thigh. As well, I'd still remain uncomfortable naked. I'd still have to avoid such things as changing in locker rooms, taking gym showers, and remaining self-conscious in a bathing suit. No, I was not going to be happy with a metoidioplasty. My research for a good surgeon and acceptable phalloplasty continued.

Phalloplasty had many complicated factors to consider. Different surgeons took graft sites from different areas of the body. Most involved taking tissue from the forearm, along with microsurgery—typically resulting in a sensate penis. Other techniques involved flaps from the groin or abdomen, with no microsurgery—typically resulting in an insensate penis. There was also the question of urethral lengthening, and extending a urethra through the new penis. Some surgeons offered this and others did not. What would I be willing to live with? What would I be willing to sacrifice?

Sadly, most information and stories on phalloplasty from the FTM community at large remained mostly negative. But as time passed, I realized most of these comments were from guys who hadn't actually had bottom surgery. Were transmen who had had bottom surgery who had poor results and complications more prone to post information? Were the guys who had positive results happy and simply moving on? I decided it was time to start consulting with surgeons in person, hoping to obtain more direct information.

For years I'd heard positive comments on a well-known GRS surgeon named Toby Meltzer who was practicing in the Southwest. But all information from FTM groups stated he no longer performed phalloplasty and was only performing metoidioplasty. Another surgeon from the Midwest seemed viable, but the cost was prohibitive at upwards of $100,000.

In 2006, I flew out to consult with a team in Europe. I felt comfortable with their long history, and what I'd seen of their results. Their fee was under $50,000, which would be manageable. The graft would be taken from the forearm, and they would perform microsurgery with the expectation of a sensate penis. The penises they created looked fairly good, and I'd be able to stand and urinate through a fully-extended urethra.

The main surgeon seemed a bit rushed during consultation, so I was not able to ask many questions. His office assistant took over and set up a slide presentation. With photos included, it described the entire procedure graphically. I then met with the urologist. He was a good-humored and friendly man who gladly answered my questions. Considering I was most nervous about the urethra work, I was comforted to find him so attentive.

The biggest drawback for me was that their procedure would involve removing a portion of the forearm. I was not sure I wanted to live with such a scar. Such sacrifice made me again question whether or not I could live with or without a penis. Leaning more toward it being worse to live without it, I was placed on their surgery wait list. In preparation, I returned home and obtained a total hysterectomy.

I then consulted by phone with a surgeon on the East Coast of the U.S. who was doing abdominal phalloplasty. His fee was under $50,000, and I'd seen a couple of his results online. Tissue would be taken from the abdomen, leaving the forearm intact. The trade-off was he did not do urethral extension, so I would not be able to stand to urinate. And with no microsurgery, the penis would be insensate. But keeping a scar-free forearm weighed strongly.

However, during our phone consultation, I became rather uncomfortable. I felt this surgeon was stretching the truth of his surgery a bit, and downplaying my concerns. The more I spoke with him, the more I felt I was talking with a car salesman.

In the meantime, I decided to call the office of Dr. Toby Meltzer because of his excellent reputation and history as a GRS surgeon to ask him if he could recommend a surgeon. His scheduler Carole answered the phone, and when I told her what I was inquiring about, she sounded rather surprised. "Dr. Meltzer does phalloplasty," she replied. I experienced a rush of shock and excitement flow through me upon hearing those words. I couldn't believe it.

As it turned out, Dr. Meltzer had stopped doing forearm grafts due to the high cost of doing so in the US, but was still performing the pedicle flap (groin/hip) phalloplasty. He also did primary urethral lengthening partially extending the urethra up toward the base of the penis, similar to how it's done in metoidioplasty. Although the urethra would remain rather short, it held the hope of standing to urinate, which filled me with even more excitement.

Carole was kind and patient to explain the details of the various procedures, and broke down the stages and fees for each of them. My excitement was surreal, and I immediately booked both a consultation and a plane ticket.

Dr. Meltzer was genuinely friendly, laid back, and intelligent. He educated me about the various phalloplasty techniques currently being performed worldwide, and told me I'd need to decide what was most important for me. He talked about his past phalloplasty work and explained why he does the procedures he currently performs. He openly shared the pros and cons of each. He answered every question I asked.

He showed me photos, and the penis looked aesthetically nice. The groin/hip donor site would leave only a single elongated line scar. The cost was going to be about $10,000 or more than the other two surgeons I'd considered, but it was still financially doable.

This was a dream come true. A surgeon whose name I trusted, a nice looking penis, a minimal scar on the hip, and primary urethral lengthening. The quest for my missing penis was transformed from a state of apprehension and uncertainty to eager anticipation for the actual surgery date to arrive.

In 2007, when the date finally arrived, I felt no fear. I'd expected I would, but the fear wasn't there. Instead, I felt indescribable gratefulness and relief. And to top things off, my health insurance approved coverage for the surgery with a cap of $75,000.

The surgery process itself was quite exhausting. Dr. Meltzer's phalloplasty was performed in stages, which required several round trip airline flights. The initial main surgery consisted of phalloplasty, vaginectomy, and primary urethral lengthening. The first thing I remember post-op was being transferred to a hospital bed from the operating room gurney and looking down, and catching a glimpse of my curved penis before someone covered it with a blanket. It looked small, though I would later find it was far from that.

The pain was as if someone had shoved a large jagged rock inside my pelvis. That was the vaginectomy, which remained painful for a good month or so. The vaginectomy was performed by a very kind and funny obstetrician who worked with Dr. Meltzer.

After a few days in the hospital, I was discharged to a hotel where I remained in town until the stent in my new urethra and the supra-pubic catheter in my bladder could both be removed. After removal of the catheters and assurance I could urinate freely, I flew home.

For several weeks the tip of my penis remained attached to my right groin (hence called "suitcase handle" because it looks just like one), allowing the penis time to establish its own blood supply from the base. After a few weeks, a "delay" was performed, where Dr. Meltzer cut a portion of the tip away from its attachment point, which encourages the penis to develop yet more of its own blood supply. After that, I performed another delay at home by tying a thin piece of silicone around the tissue still hanging on at the groin and tying it a little tighter every couple of days. Dr. Meltzer then surgically released the tip completely, and my penis was free to hang as a normal penis would. That was certainly an awesome day.

Scrotoplasty and tissue expanders were next. Two tissue expanders were placed in the scrotal sack to slowly stretch out two pockets for testicular implants to later be placed. Injection ports were placed under the skin of the groin, and each week using a needle I injected up to 10 milliliters of saline into each expander. I found it difficult to do without being a contortionist, so a dear friend performed the weekly chore for me. This was done over a couple months until each side held nearly 70 milliliters of fluid. It pretty much looked and felt as if I had two cue balls between my legs. This was not just uncomfortable towards the end, but painful because they rubbed together and against my pubic bone. It was a glorious day of relief to have them removed and replaced with the soft and relatively small testicular implants instead.

The glansoplasty, creating the glans or "head" of the penis was last. The initial length of my penis was 6.5 inches. Dr. Meltzer explained that he creates them long in the rare case of any necrosis at the tip, requiring a bit to be removed. I had no necrosis, so my penis remained 6.5 inches. During glansoplasty, I could choose to have the length trimmed down, with Dr. Meltzer suggesting a 4-inch penis. I'd become quite attached to my 6.5 inches, and knew that it would never grow any longer for intercourse. A biological penis grows as it becomes erect, but with phalloplasty, what you see is what you get. Transmen with phallos are "showers" rather than "growers." Dr. Meltzer joked that I'd have to coil it up in my underwear, and explained to me that the average flaccid penis was more like 3.5 inches. He drew markings on my penis where he suggested it be trimmed down, and took a photo so I could see how it would still appear quite long. His nurse chimed in with a wide-eyed facial expression that declared, "scary long." But to me, it looked too short. Dr. Meltzer told me it was my decision, but didn't want to see me unhappy later on. We compromised on 4.5 to 5 inches. As I began waking up at the end of surgery, the first thing he did was whisper in my ear, "Don't worry, I went on the long side."

Finally, I had my completed penis. And, was it handsome. Nothing at all like the "mangled flesh" I'd read so much about.

My surgery was free of complications, for which I feel lucky. A few minor glitches were an infection at the tip of my penis while it was still in "suit case handle" mode, but this cleared quickly with antibiotics. With the scrotoplasty, a few sutures popped open, resulting in the need to keep the opening rinsed and clean while it healed from the inside out, which it did without trouble.

My main concern going in was the primary urethral lengthening—but that was flawless, except for the fact it was short, making it difficult to clear the fly of my pants when standing to pee. So, I nearly always sat down to urinate, which was disappointing.

Hence, nearly four years later, I decided to get the urethra extended to the tip of my penis with Dr. Meltzer who had then begun doing so. For this surgery, I paid for it myself out of pocket. The procedure also allowed for the option to have every remnant of female anatomy buried into my scrotum, never to be seen again. It was a very difficult year-long road, mainly due to urethral strictures. Treatment included self-dilations with urethral dilators, repeated surgeries, and catheters. But it seems all has finally healed and I am standing to pee at urinals with the rest of the guys. An alleviating joy, so very worth the ordeal.

As time passes, I must eat crow in regards to my chosen penis length. Even a 5-inch flaccid penis is cumbersome, just as Dr. Meltzer had warned. It is quite unruly, slipping out of my underwear and traveling down my pants leg, very embarrassing. Sure, I look "hung," which may sound great, but it's not all it's cracked up to be. Sometimes I feel a little bit self-conscious about it. But, in a way, I also like being a bit on the larger side, considering I went so many years without.

Prior to phalloplasty, I avoided mirrors when naked. The worst was taking a shower, having to wash "down there," being forced to face that my genitalia was wrong. Immediately stepping from the shower, I'd wrap the towel around my waist, so as not to see a man without a penis in the mirror. I disliked getting dressed each day, the task of slipping on my prosthetic penis, knowing that it was fake and female genitalia lay underneath and worrying that it would fall out.

My main pleasures are swimming, bicycling, and working out at the gym. All of these activities were uncomfortable prior to phalloplasty. The prosthetic penis would shift when I cycled or swam, and it never looked natural in wet bathing trunks. I could never change or shower in the locker room at the gym. I always felt uncomfortable and limited in the activities I enjoyed most.

Now that I have my own flesh and blood penis, I enjoy getting dressed and wearing underwear. I also enjoy taking a shower and soaping up my "junk." I intentionally linger in front of the mirror when I'm naked now, and the reflection brings a smile of relief to see my entire body with all the right parts in all the right places. And finally, feeling the warmth of my penis tapping against my thigh when I walk, and resting against it when I sit. No longer do I rush to put clothes on to cover up.

I went body surfing at the ocean one summer and the waves were so rough they ripped my trunks to my knees. Not that I wasn't embarrassed, but hey, I had all the right parts to be embarrassed about exposing. I would have been mortified prior to surgery. I can now change clothes with the other guys at the gym, and shower in the group shower. My penis blends in with the rest of them. There's even a gay man who loves to talk to me while I'm naked in the locker room—the ultimate seal of penis approval.

Every moment of life is now much more comfortable. I am at peace knowing I can be anywhere at any time in any situation and safe and feel complete. Before phalloplasty, even years into my transition, I'd have nightmares about strangers angrily grabbing my crotch and shouting at me that I had no penis. I feel this stemmed from my own deep-seated distress over being penis-less. But those nightmares have vanished. No longer is there worry over finding myself in a situation where I may have to be nude among strangers. No sense of unease in bathrooms, changing rooms, airports, doctor's offices. Best of all, no more sense of unease when simply by myself. Phalloplasty has brought me indescribable wholeness and comfort.

As a result, my confidence in nearly everything has grown exponentially. I feel content in a way that allows me to move on with life and do anything I desire. Go anywhere I want.

I thought sex would become a matter of huge importance and desire after phalloplasty, but that has not occurred. My sex drive and sexual comfort have increased, but at the same time, phalloplasty has brought a sort of contentment to where I'm simply happier in life and happier being single. Absolutely, yes, I'm a million times more comfortable being nude in front of people, or letting someone now touch my genitals. Previously, the discomfort of such was almost sickening.

Though a pedicle flap phallo is considered insensate, I do have some tactile sensation in my penis. And due to nerves remaining intact in the prior parts, it feels like it has erotic sensation too. I'm able to orgasm easily by jacking-off my penis. I hear many guys say they aren't getting bottom surgery, particularly phalloplasty, because they fear or assume they will lose sexual feeling or function. For me, that has not been true.

Is my phalloplasty perfect? No. My penis does not become erect upon arousal. And I do not have completely normal erotic nor tactile sensation throughout my entire penis, as would most men. But am I happy with my surgery? Absolutely.

Seeing and feeling my warm and handsome penis every day brings me great peace, and a sense of almost overwhelming disbelief that I am finally complete, after so many years of waiting. Phalloplasty has been a positive, life-changing event for me. Now I often wonder how I managed to survive without it before.

Somatic Integrity

Gabriel Richardson

When I first began my medical transition, I could never have predicted just how at home I would feel in my body today. My path to transition was indirect and late in life, but worth the journey. Once I started the transition process however, I ended up on a fast track to live the rest of my life as a man.

Initially, my knowledge regarding genital reconstruction was limited. I had seen two or three photographic depictions of phalloplasty in Dean Kotula's book, *The Phallus Palace* (2002), neither of which I found inspiring, and I was vocal about my disappointment. I have since learned how harmful that was to broadcast my feelings to other trans men considering bottom surgery and to the men providing those images. To compound the issue further, I still was not identifying as a man and had no indication then that I ever would, so I felt justified in denigrating the whole process.

For a few years, prior to going on testosterone (T), I identified as trans, but still, to a certain degree, aligned myself with a more academic viewpoint of gender being socially constructed. I was uncomfortable embracing the notion that one day I would be living in the world as a man, and the thought of surgically modifying my genitals had not even entered my consciousness.

Once I learned about the prospect of hormonally altering my physical body, my primary concern became whether my personality would be altered with the introduction of *male hormones*, and if so, how and in what ways. Basically, I was worried that I would turn into an angry and violent man.

That fear, I now believe, was directly related to my understanding of what my lesbian separatist sisters had been working tirelessly since the 1970s to overthrow: the patriarchy. In retrospect, I think some of us scapegoated men and masculinity with the view that all men are the enemy. My involvement with lesbian separatists warped my own view of men. Subsequently, I had a difficult time accepting that my true inner-self was indeed male, not female. I may have been anatomically assigned female at birth, but I grew up to become an assertive male. I believe that bias espoused by my former community remains toxic to the trans male community.

In 2005, I began my medical transition: injecting testosterone on a weekly basis. A year later, I underwent chest reconstruction with Dr. Michael Brownstein in San Francisco. I feel fortunate to have begun my transition in San Francisco, because I was able to find a trans-aware physician who prescribed my testosterone without the need of a psychotherapist letter. She also did not require that my trans-narrative match the dominant discourse of trans-identity: as an example, I did not know from a young age that I was supposed to feel I was born in the wrong body. In fact, I was not at all bothered by my body. I honestly had no idea that it could be otherwise, so I accepted it the way it was. Though my body did not fit the way I felt, I did not loathe my body.

Nevertheless, I was still not convinced that genital reconstruction was a necessary or viable option for me. I had some strong, but mostly uninformed, opinions about bottom surgery. In the past I was convinced it was a misogynistic procedure that resulted from the hatred of one's femaleness. The results I had seen were nothing to brag about. Even if I had considered this surgery, I never thought that I would be able to afford such an expensive procedure anyway.

As it turned out, going forward with the full sex affirmation surgery process (chest and genital reconstruction) was directly related to my journey of actualizing my authentic self and achieving somatic integration: the ability to live more fully in my body, and the world, as a man. I had no idea how profound transition would be for me.

Because my exposure to phalloplasty procedures was limited, I could not have imagined how talented the plastic surgeon who performed my surgery would be, nor how realistic my penis would look, feel and function. I had heard many of the common remarks: *Phalloplasty provides an insensate organ barely approximating a penis*; or, *If you're going to get bottom surgery, it's better to get a metoidioplasty, because at least you'll have sensation and a natural erection, even if it is rather small.*

The biggest surprise of all was that my wife's employer provided insurance coverage for trans surgeries, to the tune of $75,000, which included airfare, lodging and a daily per diem due to the "out of network" travel to an approved surgeon.

The psychological and physical leap from chest to genital reconstruction was not a simple process for me. The emotional, financial and physical investment of top surgery seemed inevitable and necessary, if the goal was to look more male. Bottom surgery, however, did not seem as inevitable or necessary, because no one would suspect, by the way I looked and sounded, that I did not already have a penis. I was sure that there would never be a good enough reason to pursue it any further.

Then in 2007, I attended *Gender Odyssey,* an annual conference in Seattle, WA. The audience was primarily FTMs. I attended a workshop, which provided post-transition trans men a chance to discuss issues, exclusively affecting them. Since I had only been on T for a couple of years, I was part of the audience instructed to listen rather than participate.

The issues the post-transition guys dealt with seemed so different from those with which I was dealing. For instance, they talked about the pressures they experienced from their non-trans peers regarding their intimate relationships. Some of the guys had been with the same female partner for 10 or more years but were not "married," and their colleagues wanted to know why. Most of the men were stealth, and thus could not explain that they were unable to marry legally, until recently, in some localities. Their non-trans colleagues, especially the females, considered them commitment phobic.

None of the trans men in the workshop spoke about completing genital reconstruction, yet several spoke about the regret they felt, because they had not pursued the surgery, which I found informative. I listened as these trans men described awkward moments in their male bonding experiences with non-trans men, which mostly involved outdoor activities like hiking, biking, swimming and hot-tubbing. For example, many of them described going on long outdoor excursions that were physically demanding and required lots of water to stay hydrated, yet they had limited access to restrooms: this turned out to be a true hardship and barrier for them. They shared how difficult it was to be the only guy (in a group of males) who always needed to find a bathroom to relieve himself. And other men complained of how their soft "packie" floated around in their swimming trunks whenever they went into the water.

Beyond the physical demands, the men described the emotional toll that not having a penis took on their romantic and social lives. I remember hearing one man speaking about how in the first few years of his transition he felt like he had been convinced having a penis was unnecessary, because he met so many trans men who told him that "the penis does not make the man," yet he ended up feeling otherwise. He eventually did come to feel that in order for him to live more fully as a man, he needed to have a penis, but he felt like the most opportune time had passed him by: he believed he was now too old, too broke and too sick. He was angry that so many of his trans-brothers had dissuaded him from seriously considering the procedure, considering the importance it would end up being for him. He questioned why these men had cared so much about the issue, why had they felt the need to criticize other trans men who opted for genital reconstruction. He wondered how they could be experts on a topic they had never experienced personally.

I walked away from that workshop determined to research the various surgeries and surgeons available, the cost, and how I would need to proceed with my health insurance to move forward. I did not want to end up regretting not taking advantage of the opportunity while I still had the chance.

I spent months compiling research. I found some Yahoo discussion groups that focused on the topic, where I also encountered the phalloplasty vs. metoidioplasty debate and anti-phalloplasty rhetoric. Again, this was mostly from people who had completed *neither* procedure. It was during this time that I became aware of the impact of the pervasive bottom surgery negative-talk that seems to exist in the FTM and broader trans community. Early in my transition, I had contributed to that negative conversation through my biased comments made to friends and participants in FTM meetings.

After many conversations with trans men, I have concluded that many of those trans men, who have completed the phalloplasty or metoidioplasty process, remove themselves from the online groups and/or community, leaving the remaining members without the benefit of their words of encouragement, caution and experience. The way criticism is currently expressed in the trans male community is neither helpful nor constructive, but rather is demoralizing and divisive. Men who have had phalloplasty or metoidioplasty feel marginalized and alienated from the community. The impact on the men, who have not pursued phalloplasty or metoidioplasty, is a skewed understanding of the process and the results.

I settled on phalloplasty over metoidioplasty, because I was not gifted with much natural growth from the use of testosterone. But I still needed to decide between the forearm, pedicle flap, abdominal, or MLD surgery options. My health care provider would only pay for medical coverage in the United States, so I focused on Dr. Toby Meltzer in Arizona, Dr. Lawrence Gottlieb in Illinois, Dr. Sherman Leis in Pennsylvania, and Dr. Neal Wilson in Michigan. I met some guys at FTM events and conferences who were willing to show me the results of their surgeries, and I also contacted the surgeons. With all the information I received, the next step was to inform my physician that I was ready to attend a consultation with two surgeons: Dr. Leis and Dr. Meltzer.

Dr. Sherman Leis had a trans surgery center in Philadelphia, Pennsylvania and Dr. Toby Meltzer had one in Scottsdale, Arizona. Since I lived in California, Arizona seemed like a much better option for making several trips for a multi-stage surgical procedure. Still, I wanted to have a consultation with both doctors. I met with Dr. Leis in Tucson where he was a workshop presenter at the 2008 International Federation for Gender Education (IFGE) conference. I attended Dr. Leis' workshop focusing on FTM surgeries: both top and bottom. I was impressed with his craftsmanship, except for the glans portion. Although the appearance of a glans was created using a form of scarification, his procedure did not actually provide one with raised edges.

At the IFGE conference, I also had the good fortune of meeting a trans man, who had already completed phalloplasty with Dr. Meltzer, and was willing to show me the results. What I saw surprised me! His penis looked just like a non-trans man's penis. It was pinkish, about 5 inches long and had a well formed glans, with raised edges. I knew right then that I would be selecting Dr. Meltzer, but I still needed to go through the formality of a consultation, per my health care provider's instructions.

In September 2008, I had my consultation with Dr. Meltzer in Seattle, where he held a workshop on FTM surgeries similar to the one Dr. Leis had presented. Since I was already impressed with Dr. Meltzer's workmanship, once we talked specifics about the procedures in a private hotel room, I informed him that I would be selecting him as my surgeon. I was informed that he had a recent surgery cancellation and that October 18th was available so I booked it. Immediately following the consultation, I called my wife to tell her the good news.

Dr. Meltzer's colleague, a gynecologist, Dr. Webb, performed the hysterectomy, oophorectomy, and vaginectomy, while Dr. Meltzer performed the first stage of the pedicle-flap phalloplasty. My surgery was expected to last approximately five hours and I was told to stay in town for 12 days for maximum healing benefit. Fortunately, my insurance provider paid for a traveling companion so my wife accompanied me to Arizona. A close family friend joined my wife in the surgical waiting room, which turned out to be a good idea since my surgery ended up taking ten hours. Dr. Webb informed me later that my uterus was unusually large and rather difficult to remove laparoscopically, but he had taken the additional time in order to spare me the extensive scarring and additional healing time that another procedure would have required.

I spent two nights in the recovery room of a local surgery center and then stayed for 12 days at a Holiday Inn Express. Having my wife with me proved to be an invaluable component of my aftercare success. The gift of the caretaker is that they can assist with everything. I needed help getting to the bathroom, getting dressed, bathing, preparing food, replacing bandages, applying ointments and taking medications. The sensitive nature of the process was much easier to navigate with my wife, than it would have been with a friend or acquaintance.

Dr. Meltzer and/or one of his nurses came to visit me regularly in my hotel room to check on my healing progress and pain level and restock my supply of bandages, tape and ointments. I felt cared for, which allowed me to relax and heal more rapidly. About a week post-op, I began taking walks to the surgery center, two blocks away, to spend time with other men, healing from the same surgery as me, where I learned that many of them did not have the luxury of a traveling companion, which meant that they had to be much more self-sufficient. They were unable to relax as much, which undoubtedly impacted their healing time. I felt fortunate by comparison.

A few years have passed since that first genital surgery was performed, and only now am I able to attempt to articulate how the surgery has affected my sense of male embodiment (physically, socially, sexually, and spiritually), and how I express and experience my masculinity. I am convinced, more and more, with each passing day that I made the right decision for me. Going forward with the surgery has provided me with an insight into my psyche that I might not otherwise have discovered. I was male-identified before the surgery, but now I identify as a man, which turns out to be a very different form of consciousness and embodiment for me.

This realization brings me back full circle to where I began: my hesitance to transition and overcome social constructs of men as misogynists. I feel at home in my body now, in a way I never have before. The phalloplasty was the catalyst for a radical paradigm shift in my way of thinking about men and my own male identity. Having a penis has moved me from a trans embodiment and identity to a purely male one. I now know what it feels like to embody somatic integration: where my mind, body, spirit and experience have all aligned to provide me with a truly amazing life, marriage, career and network of loving people.

My life is not perfect now. Many new paths challenge me that I must learn to navigate, since I am accepted unquestioningly as a man. For instance, I have experienced a sharp learning curve with sex and the mechanics of it, which I had assumed would be easy: insert A into B. I have found it to be otherwise. One aspect of genital reconstruction surgery, which I had not taken into consideration, is the time-frame of the stages and all of the subsequent healing time. I had my initial surgery in October 2008, and it wasn't until March 2010 that I was completely healed and ready for regular sexual activity.

The prospect of engaging in open discussion with my partner about how, when and where to make love was easy pre-op, but I have found it more challenging post-op. I believe I experienced a de-sexualization of my genitals through the surgery stages and healing process. My junk was swollen, red, bloody, scabby, irritated, disfigured and sore for weeks at a time, and needed careful application of ointments and bandages, which my wife was lovingly willing to assist with. Nevertheless, I went two years with little sexual activity. So when the opportunity presented itself, I felt shy and uncomfortable. Never a strap-on kind of guy, I was unfamiliar with penis/vagina sex, so I not only felt inadequate, I was less talented at performing well, which had *never* been an issue for me before.

Because I have not yet had an erection device implanted, I must make due with a layering technique I learned from another trans guy, which creates enough rigidity for penetration. It involves wrapping one layer of 3M Coban self-adhesive bandage (like an ace bandage but thinner) and applying two condoms, which creates sufficient rigidity for penetration. Unfortunately, this also means that I do not feel as much sensation so I am eager to move forward with getting this next stage of surgery.

However, two other unanticipated issues have arisen. First, spontaneity is currently not a guarantee, and secondly, I discovered that I had unconsciously defined former, enjoyable sex acts with my wife as "lesbian sex," sex that *only* occurs between two females. I think the shift happened for me post-phalloplasty, since I no longer had genitals considered female. Now that I am a straight man with a penis, I want to have sex like a straight man, which, for me, means penis/vagina penetrative sex.

Both of these issues have caused interruptions in my marriage, but unlike the spontaneity issue, which is a bummer, but manageable, the redefinition of sex acts caused a deeper, more emotional, distance between my wife and myself. The unconscious and unspoken change in my mindset caused her to begin doubting her sexiness, attractiveness and desirability. None of which were issues for me, but that was unclear to her since I was not able to verbalize my thoughts and feelings until becoming aware of them, which took several months.

The primary issue was that I had designated certain sex acts inappropriate for a male/female couple, and therefore to be avoided. The lack of spontaneity, lack of erotic sensation from the wrapping, and my performance anxiety all combined to make the situation seem too cumbersome to negotiate. The trouble with this is that I had begun to initiate sex less and less to the point of not at all.

I was able to justify this stance in my own mind for months. Then I had an epiphany. I realized exactly what I was doing to myself, my wife, and our marriage. Thankfully, I *did* come to realize the implications of my actions and had a heart-to-heart talk with my wife, which went well and provided us with another avenue for deepening our love and commitment for each other. One suggestion that came from our dialogue was the idea of seeing a sex therapist as a couple, which we decided would be a wonderful way to re-invest in our marriage.

My life is still not perfect, but it is ideal. It has been worth each and every twist and turn it has taken.

Before and After

Cinque

After being on hormones for six months, I felt like I was in gender/ sex limbo, suspended between feeling and being seen as a man but unable to fully express my male identity. But deciding to have genital surgery moved me out of this mind-body prison, and I felt immediate relief knowing that I would be able to make love to my wife the way I had always wanted to. I would be able to stand and urinate with other men and not be continually reminded of my anatomical difference from them when I went to the bathroom. I also looked forward to being a part of conversations with other guys when the topic turned to sex instead of feeling like a silent bystander with little to contribute and relate to. I would no longer be the kid who flipped through the Sears catalog daydreaming about things that I would never have. I was finally going to feel complete as the man I had always known myself to be.

Then suddenly my dreams came to a screeching halt when I received devastating news four days before my scheduled departure to Serbia. The test results from my Hepatitis C and HIV screening had come back positive. I was shocked and dumbfounded that this could happen in the 11th hour when I was so close to realizing my dream. I had worked hard to save the money while biding my time feeling like half a man. I was only inches from the finish line. I collapsed on the bedroom floor and sobbed uncontrollably. My wife did her best to comfort me. I felt so despondent. Looking back now, I am surprised that my response was not about the test results themselves, but rather about the prospect that my surgery would be canceled and that no surgeon would want to operate on me. I thought that I would have to live the rest of my life in a liminal space of no man's land.

After a solid fifteen minutes of bawling, I collected myself and began wondering if the surgeons would make an exception in my case. Then it suddenly occurred to me that something was seriously wrong. I had never engaged in the kinds of sexual or social behaviors associated with contracting HIV or Hepatitis C. I had never slept with men, or had a blood transfusion, or used IV drugs. Nor had I slept with any women who were HIV+. I phoned my doctors and explained the situation, and they told me to come regardless because they didn't discriminate against people. The test was simply a formality that helped them plan their surgical approach. My spirits soared again, and a second test showed that the first results had been wrong.

Decisions

When I initially transitioned bottom surgery was not on my radar screen. I was a little curious about phalloplasty however. But most of what I read in books and on the internet was disparaging and discouraging. The way people talked about post-op genitals was horrifying. Social pressure also affected some of my transition decisions. I was sensitive to sentiments in our queer community about the loss of so many butches who were transitioning in increasing numbers. I also tried to stay in a liminal gender space for my wife who was and still is a lesbian and feminist. I was concerned about how my transition would affect how people treated her in our own community, where there had been tensions and conflicts between trans folks and cis-gendered lesbians, as well as in dominant, normative contexts, where her queer identity would be overlooked and rendered invisible.

About year after chest surgery and six months of testosterone, I started feeling a deep, seismic shift in both my gender consciousness and sexed embodiment. Testosterone had masculinized my body with muscle, hair growth (and loss), structural facial changes, a thickening trachea and deeper voice. Skin that had been smooth became coarse and furrier. My body was moving past gender fluidity and sexual ambiguity. Chest reconstruction and weight-lifting had changed breasts into male pectorals. All these changes seemed to build on one another. They felt cumulative as I continued transitioning medically, and were the basis for that seismic gender shift unfurling in my mind and body. My round face squared into an angular jaw, which exploded in hair growth that coarsened after a couple of years.

While I enjoyed the masculinization of my body, the changes also brought forth new problems of feeling limited in my body. While hormones and chest surgery made the men's bathroom accessible, I also had to confront my anatomical difference from other men. Being unable to stand and void was a painful, constant reminder of my physical and social difference from them.

Not having a penis also hindered how much I could bond with other men. It was difficult to fully participate in many social activities. I had to think about how to deal with certain things ahead of time and sometimes couldn't participate at all, depending on the circumstances. In swimming pools and hot tubs, I had to be aware that my prosthetic might start floating around and looking unnatural in my swim trunks. When I worked out or played ball with the guys, I had to make excuses for why I couldn't shower with the team or disrobe in the gym. On hiking trips, I got tired of being the guy who always needed to find a tree to relieve myself. I was also uncomfortable going into the steam room at the gym and to bath spas where I could relax and hang out with other guys. Feeling these restrictions constantly reminded me of my anatomical difference from my natal buddies on a daily basis. Eventually, the emotional burden became too heavy to bear. I wanted to relax and be a man without having to manage myself all the time. I had changed most of my physical sex characteristics, but still had the nagging problem of my genitals, which was increasingly contradicting my gender embodiment. I could no longer pretend that my genitals were irrelevant to my gender. It felt like a drive deep from within the cortical layers of my brain to change and complete my sex.

I also became concerned about my safety, especially because I travel a lot. Since transitioning, I notice that people treat me a lot differently now, especially cops, customs officers, and border patrol. Depending on the context and person(s), I get pegged as a thug, criminal, undocumented worker, or terrorist. To make matters worse, three of my friends had horrible experiences of being strip-searched by TSA officers and border patrolmen. All of them described their fear and humiliation in vivid detail. They felt like they had been singled out because of their race and ethnicity. The same thing was beginning to happen to me when I traveled out of the country. Being so vulnerable and exposed all the time became unbearable. I had to find a solution.

I went to Serbia for MLD phalloplasty for several reasons. Serbia was the cheapest place in the world for phalloplasty that I was aware of at the time. My surgery cost roughly $50,000 for everything, including the surgery itself, travel, lodging, hospital, and medication. I was also attracted to their MLD procedure, which has a unique architecture and produces good looking, sturdy penises. Professor Sava Perovic had been doing the procedure since 1995, which meant that they had plenty of time to work out the kinks and complications. In addition to harvesting nerves, arteries, and blood vessels, this procedure took muscle tissue from the lat muscle in my back. This meant that my penis would have a meaty girth. I liked some of the results of the free flap forearm procedure also, but I didn't want to sacrifice my arm. Nor did my arms have enough tissue for the size of penis that I imagined for myself. My forearms have less sensitivity than my back, which always had a lot of erotic sensitivity. Many years of working construction and cooking in kitchens had damaged and desensitized the nerves in my forearms. I searched all over North America for a surgeon who could perform phalloplasty for a price I could afford, but found none. The Professor and his protégé, Dr. Rados Djinovic, also had superb microsurgery skills and stellar reputations.

(Re)made in Serbia

I started surgery in July 2009 with Professor Perovic and Dr. Djinovic in Belgrade, but the Professor died in April 2010 and Dr. Djinovic took over the practice. I was not worried about having surgery in Serbia. The wars of the 1990s had long concluded, and I found Belgrade to be like other European cities. It has a social scene and vibrant culture and hardworking people with a long history of achievements in science, medicine, and engineering. The hospitals and medical facilities are modern, and since healthcare in Serbia is socialized, my hospital costs were a fraction of what they would have been in the U.S.

I had a wonderful personable relationship with my doctors and nurses. They treated me very well, and I felt embraced like a fellow countryman. I found them to be accepting, genuine, and approachable. I was impressed by my doctors' surgical and artistic abilities and genuine good will to help trans people. I was also touched by their humility and down-to-earth manner. They took considerable time to answer all of my questions about surgery, and money was a secondary concern. In fact, I had to remind my doctors on two occasions to collect payment for surgery. They were more focused on producing the best results than on making lots of money. I also didn't feel that professional barrier separating patient from doctor which I've felt from other doctors. My surgeons sat down beside me, looked me in the eye and talked *with* me rather that *at* me. Because they were so laid back and down-to-earth, I found it easy to entrust them with my body and life. The nurses also took excellent care of me. They were very gentle, constantly checked on me, and attended to all my needs.

My surgery took four trips, and I was blessed to have only two complications through the entire process. The first difficulty was my donor site closing completely. There was a small pocket of infection—likely caused by a stitch that didn't fully dissolve—in the area that prevented the wound from fully healing. The other problem came at the end when my right testicle became infected and had to be removed. I think I may have brought on the infection by being active before I had completely healed. It's always been hard for me to lie around and do nothing. Dr. Djinovic re-implanted the testicle when I returned to Serbia a final time for a few cosmetic touch-ups.

I began regaining sensation in my penis about four months after the first surgery. It was exhilarating. I had always had a mental construct of my penis since childhood, but for the first time, I was actually feeling it as flesh of my body. I marveled at the wonders of medical genius. However, while I had a mental construct, it still took a while for me to grow into my penis. It wasn't immediate right after surgery. In the first few weeks post-op, my penis felt like an attachment to my groin, because the fleshly connections were still cementing at the cellular level. I was aware of my penis as I held it in my hand and could feel it connected to my groin when I tugged on it. I could feel it in my briefs, warm and lying against my thigh. While I was aware of my penis as a part of my body, my consciousness in it had not yet fully taken hold. By October, however, the nerves started regenerating on both the surface and inside of my penis and spreading up the shaft. By November, the nerve connections had cemented, and the connections between my flesh and consciousness had gelled completely and felt fully integrated and seamless.

This is when I began feeling my consciousness expand (and move) into my penis as a natural part of my body/self. The initial feeling of something being attached to my body gave way to a new feeling of fleshly completion and fully inhabiting every inch of my skin. The most surprising development of my journey was being unable, in just four months after surgery, to conjure a (body) memory of my pre-op genitalia and gender embodiment. I did not expect that in such a short span of time, I would come to feel like my penis had always been there all along. This had also occurred with top surgery in which, in less than a week post-op, I was unable to recall having had flesh attached to my chest for 35 years! I was surprised at how quickly my (body) memory of female body parts faded as a result of testosterone and surgery.

I had a total of seven surgeries. For each surgical phase, there were post-op care instructions to follow in order to optimize the results and prepare my body for the next stage. The first two operations were the longest and most painful. My doctors removed all the old reproductive plumbing, cut and sculpted my penis from my back, and attached it to my groin. I hear they have simplified these two procedures into one operation now. After this, I had to keep the underside of my penis moist with ointment for five months until returning to Serbia for the second phase for urethraplasty and scrotoplasty. It actually took two more trips to Belgrade to make my urethra and scrotum.

After urethraplasty, I had to catheterize for a few weeks post-op to keep the channel from closing while the tissue healed. On returning home from the final surgery in which the erectile prosthesis was implanted, I also had to keep my penis erect for almost a month so that the tissue would heal properly around the prosthesis. I combined holidays with vacation time to get time off from work to recover. I needed a month to recover from the first and last surgeries because they were the hardest and made mobility virtually impossible.

I wanted to finish this part of my transition as quickly as possible and was blessed to get through it in only 16 months. It was an intense marathon of medicalization and transatlantic travel that required a lot of mental stamina, faith, and trust in the goodness of others to help when I needed it. After getting through each stage, I felt grateful for the gains I had made. But eventually the novelty wore off, and I would start looking to the next stage and anticipating what it would bring. After the first surgery, for example, I was happy to feel flesh attached to my groin and weight in my shorts, even though my junk didn't look like a penis yet. I felt ecstatic finally to have my penis and feel different sensations and my consciousness slowly expand into it. But when I reached the point where it felt like my penis had always been there all along, then I started yearning to use the urinal with other men. While I no longer felt anatomically different from other men, I still felt functionally different. Although I had felt this way before phalloplasty, having a penis magnified my feelings of urgency. I became impatient and wanted to move on from this stage. When my urethral connection was complete and I was able to stand and void finally, I felt an overwhelming sense of delight and accomplishment.

I had crossed a major milestone in my journey. My sex, my maleness, was finally materializing on my body, and I was starting to feel like one of the guys. However, the exhilaration began wearing off after a few months, and I started lamenting that I couldn't yet have an erection and make love to my wife like I wanted. Curious, I tried to imagine what it might feel like to have my sexual desire extending literally and powerfully out of my groin. This only added to my frustration of not being able to become erect. While having a penis made me feel complete and no longer different anatomically from other men, I was still functionally different as a sexually impotent man. This was depressing and demeaning, not to mention constraining. The experience gave me insight and compassion for men who suffer from erectile dysfunction. I came to empathize with men who couldn't get an erection and understand the tremendous loss of sexual pleasure, self-esteem, and emotional connection they suffer.

Before and After

Having come so far in my journey and finally feeling complete, I look back and wonder how I actually made it through all those years in a body that was so different and at odds with my male identity. It was hard to truly express myself socially and sexually inside a female body, regardless of how masculine I felt and presented. To survive the contradiction between my gender identity and sex embodiment, I thought of myself as male and part of the social category of men. I tried to convince myself that the differences—whether physical, social, emotional, or somatic—between myself and male-bodied men (trans and nontrans) were minimal, culturally constructed, and overstated. I downplayed and glossed over these differences by performing masculinity and convincing myself that this performance was the only real thing about masculinity and male identity that mattered. I wore men's clothes, worked in traditionally male jobs, had only male roommates, and adopted men's behavioral and emotional patterns. At the same time, I had mistakenly assumed that being a butch female was the same as living as a man, and that if I could perform masculinity well enough in a butch body, I could be content. I didn't understand until transitioning medically just how important my physical body was/is in my ability to express my male identity. I have learned, however, that masculinity and maleness are expressed (and feel) differently in bodies, depending on their hormones and body parts. Hormones and surgery have made a significant difference in my feelings and the way I live today. I think back now at my naiveté in thinking that performing masculinity was the same as being in a male body. They are radically different on many levels.

When my body masculinized, doors of camaraderie opened up with other men that had been shut prior to transitioning. As a butch lesbian, I had always been close to men and found them easier to live with. But I also knew that there were things that men did and talked about amongst themselves that I was not privy to because of my female body and their social training. This changed with transition but with a paradoxical twist. I had gained entrance into those conversations and social spaces with other men that had been previously impenetrable. It felt good to be recognized and accepted by other men. But on another level, I also felt how the lower half of my body still limited me from fully participating and enmeshing myself in men's world. I felt uncomfortable undressing in locker rooms and I never used the showers or hot tubs. Conversations about sex were largely off limits also. I couldn't speak from experience like other men and couldn't relate to theirs. Listening to other men talk about sex also piqued my curiosity of what it would feel to have a penis permanently attached. I began imagining how much more intense orgasms might be if I could feel the warm pulsating vibrations of my partner's vaginal muscles contracting around my penis. As the hormone continued to make my clitoris grow, sexual desire and orgasms also became more intense than before. But again, this was a mixed blessing of being both excited and frustrated, because, while my arousal was so much more intense, my clitoris was inadequate to express the heightened intensity of my desire. It was too small and incapable of carrying such a large load. Somewhere I read that the clitoris is seen as homologous to the penis in medical science and came to see it as an undeveloped penis that could be fixed like any other unwanted urological issue.

Other differences include how I experience sex differently now than when I used a strap-on dildo. For years I had assumed that strap-on sex was the same as sex with a penis, but I could not have been more wrong. Having my penis attached to my body means that I can relax into having intercourse and not be concerned that something's going to come off track as with the strap-on. It also means I can enjoy the sensation of penetration. There is a sensory feedback loop between the nerve sensations in the shaft of my penis and my brain. Unlike before, I can now feel the warmth, softness, and moisture of my partner's body when I make love to her. I can also feel her vaginal muscles contracting, which, in combination with the intensifying heat and lubrication, is exciting! In addition to feeling my own pleasure, I can feel her pleasure now and feel myself give her pleasure. This wasn't possible before because obviously strap-ons lack the sensation and hardwire connection to my brain. Maneuvering to keep the base aligned with my clitoris to get some stimulation was always distracting and made it hard to lose myself in the moment. When I did cut loose and give way to my desire, the cock would sometimes pop out of the harness and interrupt my flow. Sex is so much more uninhibited and intense now that the strap-on is out of the picture. I can lose myself in the heat of the moment without concern.

Having a new organ meant that I had to learn how to urinate again. It also meant that I had to relearn how to masturbate and find my center of pleasure again. I had to relearn how to work my penis to pleasure my wife in intercourse and have an orgasm myself. My learning curve was steep because I had no frame of reference from which to compare my new embodiment. Surgery had combined with testosterone to rewire my erotic circuitry and redraw my erogenous zones. My doctors made a nicely shaped penis with length and girth that has three different kinds of sensation. I feel sensation both internally and externally throughout most of the shaft when it is squeezed. I also have tactile sensation on the skin surface which is still growing in. My doctors say that sensation continues growing in for many years after surgery. I have erotic sensation from where my clitoris (also still growing) was entwined in the pathway of the erectile prosthesis at the base of my penis. When I am turned on sexually, blood flows into my (already enlarged) clitoris to enlarge it further and increase its connection and sensitivity to the prosthesis. I use the erectile pump to push fluid into the cylinders implanted in the shaft of my penis to stiffen it. The pumped up cylinders connect to the enlarged clitoris to create a powerful erotic feeling when pushed, squeezed, or stroked.

Lovemaking feels more sacred now and has deepened my emotional bond with my wife. My penis feels more special than my hands or mouth, which I still use of course. But I am not limited to or by them anymore. The difference is that my hands and mouth are body parts that I share with other people, and they have other functions besides giving sexual pleasure. Also, I never got past the fact that strap-ons are manufactured products, which made it difficult to personalize them as my own organ and eventually became a significant stumbling block as I continued transitioning medically. While my penis is also man-made, it is *organic* and made from my own flesh and blood. It hasn't been produced in a factory, displayed in catalogs and sex shops, and handled by people I don't know. And no one sees or touches it without my consent. So when I make love to my wife now, sex has an added quality of sacred giving that is impossible to feel with the strap-on. I feel like I am giving a personal, sacred part of myself to her that has not been handled by strangers.

I have a better understanding of virility now and am less critical of the concept than before. I used to think of virility as a display of male bravado, arrogance, or cockiness. But medical transitioning has allowed me to experience virility from a different physical embodiment and to rethink some of those previous assumptions. There is something very self-satisfying and assuring in being able to feel my desire extend outwardly from my body, see it jut out so powerfully, and touch its fleshly reality. I couldn't do or even imagine this before transitioning. It started becoming imaginable when I began the hormone and got stronger after the reproductive organs were removed and vagina sutured. But it wasn't until I was able to see and feel my erection, including pleasuring my partner, that I felt virile and had a better understanding of what it was.

One practical advantage of having a medically engineered penis permanently attached to my body is that I don't have to carry it around or figure out how to conceal it in my pants anymore. Sex, especially public sex, is more spontaneous and enjoyable as a result. I can also enjoy lovemaking in a more carefree way without worrying that something is going to come apart and spoil the moment. Unlike bio males, moreover, I did not have to rely on genetics, luck, or prayer for endowment. I got the opportunity to choose my size, look, and functionality. I can also have an erection immediately, and it will stand as long as I like. I will never have to rely on Viagra or feel pressure, frustration, embarrassment, or deflation that men suffering from erectile dysfunction often feel. My prosthesis has a lifetime guarantee, and should it malfunction in the future, my doctors will implant another one for a few hundred dollars. I also don't have to worry about getting my wife getting pregnant or pulling out before ejaculating. Nor does she have to use birth control. We can be more carefree in our lovemaking than most cis-gender male-female couples in their fecund years.

I am blessed to have the financial means, opportunity, and social support to have genital surgery. I feel so much better about myself and future as a result. I have no regrets whatsoever, and, if anything, god forbid, ever happens to my penis, I would return to Serbia immediately and sacrifice my right lat to construct another one.

Transforming from Within

Paul James

I feel that bottom surgery was never really a choice for me. For as long as I remember, it was imperative that my body reflect the male whom I had always known myself to be. I never saw myself as a lesbian because I never felt female in the first place, and I had lived as a man for most of my life. I had always been masculine in my appearance and actions from the beginning, but I ran into problems in my 9th grade gym class when the teacher assigned me to the girls' locker room because my penis was not visible at the time. This was mortifying—plain and simple! It erased my deepest sense of myself as a boy, and facing the situation every day was unbearable. I wanted to kill myself. I made every excuse imaginable to avoid changing clothes for gym class. I really enjoyed physical education but changing clothes in the girl's locker room was repulsive. To have my body exposed like that in front of others destroyed what little adolescent self-esteem I had and gnawed at my soul. My teacher, who was a lesbian, was sympathetic, which was good, but I felt so alone, because even she could not understand ultimately what I was going through.

Getting expelled from school in the 11th grade was a God-send because it put me on a path of correcting my problem. I didn't need to finish high school. I was bright enough to get into college on my own merit, and I excelled academically and went on to earn two Bachelor's degrees.

Life was fine for a while in my twenties, but the issue with my congenital defect resurfaced again in my thirties. I reached a breaking point where I had to either change my body to match my mind or end my life. I knew that I wanted to live and enjoy life to the fullest like other men but my "deformity" made it difficult. There were some real limits. While I had always thought of myself as a man with a slight disfigurement, it was still hard emotionally because I did not feel complete as a man. It eventually consumed me. I thought about it every day to the point that I almost had a nervous breakdown. I was on an emotional rollercoaster with my mood swings becoming unpredictable and uncontrollable. I went from feeling intense rage to exhausting depression in a span of minutes, which was unusual for me. I had always been an emotionally composed person for most of my life. These feelings consumed so much of my mental energy that I had to do something.

The biggest challenge and reward was telling my family that I was going to proceed with sex reassignment. They were not shocked. In fact, they were supportive. I had heard many horror stories about people's families abandoning them, but my family has remained supportive of me and my decision.

My wife and I have always thought of me as having been born with a congenital defect. She has been supportive of me through some tough times. We discussed radial forearm phalloplasty as a possibility a few years earlier, and we felt that it was not the best route for me to take. She liked my decision to try the MLD procedure, but reminded me that she has always been in love with *me* rather than what's between my legs.

The Journey

I considered other types of surgery but after a great deal of research, I decided to go with MLD free flap phalloplasty. Function, sexual gratification, aesthetics, time duration, physical health toll, and finances were all important concerns. I considered the free flap forearm procedure, but I did not want a large visible scar on my forearm or suffer possible nerve damage. This pushed me to research other options. I wanted a good size penis that I would feel good about, and that would be fully functional for sex and voiding. So I chose the MLD surgery. Despite the large scar on my left side and lack of muscle tone underneath, I am glad I went through the process, because I got everything that I wanted.

In addition to my ethnicity, cost and financing also factored into my final decision. If I can get the same quality merchandise for less money someplace else, then that's where I am going to go for my penis. I am also Italian and our men are known to have sizeable penises, so I would not be comfortable with a smaller penis. So that ruled out metoidioplasty as a possibility. I needed a completely functional penis with ample girth and length.

While having a penis has given me a profound sense of bodily integrity, social security, and mental stability, I also paid a heavy price. The healing process was long, drawn out, and, at times, strenuous, which was hard to endure. I had complications in every stage. A hematoma developed in my right oblique after the first phase. It formed because my surgeon removed a lot of muscle from my back to form my penis. Two drains collected blood from the area during my recovery in Belgrade. These were removed during the course of my stay, but on the flight home, the swelling and the pain increased. I was still bleeding internal but didn't know it. When I got home twenty-four hours later, I had to go to my local hospital where they drained the blood and relieved the pressure. The doctors implanted another drain that remained in my side for another five weeks, which was an immensely painful ordeal. My oblique was tight for more than a year, despite stretching daily. It has improved since, but sometimes I still have a little difficulty fully expanding my lungs to breathe because of the tightness. A section of condensed skin and fat underneath still needs to be removed. Right now, it feels like a flattened tennis ball is under my arm, and, at times, it can press along my artery and become painful.

Major complications occurred in the second phase, which might have been avoided if the doctors had waited a few more months to do the procedure. In this phase, my urethra was supposed to be formed in the shaft of my penis. But a lot went wrong and after surgery my penis looked like an Oscar Myer Weiner that had been roasted over a campfire. Aside from the usual red and black bruising, blisters formed all over it, including one that ran the entire length of my shaft. Swelling continued after surgery and the catheter inside my urethra eventually pushed through the sutures and seam and burst open.

Only a small section, about 25 percent of my penis healed correctly in this second stage. My surgeons later explained that they should have waited longer until my body had healed more from the first procedure. I would have gladly waited and come back at a later time when my body was fully healed to avoid that additional pain and suffering. As it turned out, I had to return seven months later to have the procedure redone. I think they learned something as a result of my experience, because they had to change the standard surgery procedure to customize my urethra.

After my first phase, I was a little concerned about the aesthetics and functioning. But now, after my urethra has been extended and testicles and erectile pump implanted, I am much happier with the overall results. I still need glansoplasty to form the head on my penis. I had a small fistula that was repaired once and then later returned. This needs to be fixed also. For the moment, I have to hold my finger over the fistula when I urinate.

The nursing staff was attentive to all my needs and the doctors were genuinely concerned about my overall health. I felt safe in Serbia. The language barrier made communication challenging sometimes. Some of the nurses spoke little English and I did not know the Serbian language. I still managed to get my point across using facial expressions along with hand and body gestures. I was fortunate in the first phase to have a roommate who spoke English and Croatian. He had grown up in Serbia as a child so he spoke the language fluently and translated my words to the nurses and doctors.

We found that we had a lot in common. It was nice to share conversation with another human being with a life like mine. This was special for me. Transmen seem so hidden in every day society. We hide well enough that we put chameleons to shame. I met another patient, a professor, and we talked all night long into the morning and got little sleep during the day. This drove some of the nurses crazy, not because we were loud or keeping other patients awake, but because we needed to sleep so that our bodies could heal.

I experienced loss in many forms along the way. I have always been physically active, but I lost some mobility and function and was unable to exercise for extended periods of time. I lost muscle density, which affected me as a farmer. The surgeries affected my ability to do work on the farm and help my wife run our daycare business. My doctors said that I would be able to play sports after about three weeks post-op, but healing took longer because of the infections and complications. Two months after the first stage, I was still bedridden with tubes draining blood from the donor site. I had to eat rich food to create healthy blood and tissue growth to heal that area, which resulted in weight gain and affected my emotional stability. Falling behind in my responsibilities, gaining weight and not having an outlet all made me feel useless and helpless—like I was a burden to others. In some of my "down" moments I questioned if it was worth this much pain and suffering, even though I knew deep down that I had made the right choice.

On this journey, there have been moments of feeling enlivened with pure joy and amazement interwoven with stressful periods of fear and anxiety. I worried about what might happen. Will I survive? Will I ever see my wife again? Will my penis function? Will I be in even worse condition?

It took every ounce of my spiritual reserves to stay focused on healing and remain mentally positive. At times, I had to conjure a psychic connection with my lady for mental clarity and spiritual strength while I was in Belgrade recovering. When I felt troubled, I tried to imagine her face, eyes, voice, and our connection, which calmed me. I missed my wife. We are soul mates and being away from her while being hospitalized in a foreign country was the most difficult part of my journey. We have been together for twenty-three years and, prior to the surgeries, we had never spent more than a night apart when I had out-of-town jobs. Spiritually, when I was in the hospital hemorrhaging, I saw my guardian angel. It was thoughts of my wife and my guardian angel that pulled me through it all.

On the other hand, I felt overwhelming joy, wonder, and excitement when I actually saw my penis for the first time. It was a feeling of self-possession—a great gift from God. I felt as if the world had stopped momentarily and I was sitting squarely on top of it. Not to sound like Frankenstein, but my thought after surgery was: "It's alive and it's all me!" I did not care that my penis was bruised and swollen from surgery the night before. What mattered most was that it was real and part of my *own* flesh. Being able to touch and hold my penis in my hands was exhilarating, despite the severe pain and trauma. I had another moment of pure joy when my lady and I had sex for the first time post-op. Relating sexually is amazing because it is all me—my body, my penis—that satisfies my lady. When I began penetrating my wife, she started crying and I panicked, thinking that I had hurt her. When I asked what was wrong, she told me that she was so overwhelmed with happiness and joy to have *all* of me inside of her now. We shared tears of joy and gratitude. It has been a rewarding emotional journey for both of us and it deepened our connection.

I find that I am more comfortable with life and people now. I am more outgoing and want to socialize with others more. I have a much better relationship with my body, which is in tune with how I have always felt internally. This new comfort level has brought fulfillment and satisfaction. I feel like I can live fully now. Looking at my body in the mirror before surgery only brought anguish, disgust, and anger. At low points, sometimes I had considered taking my own life just to destroy the body that I saw staring back at me. I used to avoid mirrors and didn't even *consider* looking at myself naked, I feel energized when I see my reflection staring back at me now. I am so pleased with my body now. I feel more secure in public places though I am still a bit cautious in some circumstances when I need to disrobe, because my penis still needs a few more finishing touches. When I go swimming, for example, I still dress in the restroom stall, but I expect this to change when my penis is finally finished.

Having a penis allows me to feel complete and be fully integrated in my body, mind, and soul, and this allows me to express myself sexually as male. I have a lot of sensation in most of my shaft—all the way down to about an inch from the tip. (This was because my surgeon used a lot of muscle from my back to make my penis.) The physical sensation enhances my emotional and spiritual connection with my wife. I no longer have to imagine how far I am penetrating her. Now, I can actually feel her around my penis, which heightens the intensity of my emotional connection. Before surgery, we couldn't imagine how our lives would be impacted, but the surgery has helped deepen our connection and brought us even closer together.

Success is the Best Revenge

Dr. Hope

My story is an odd one. I am the statistically rare person whose history seems to differ from many of my trans brothers, whom I have met or read about. Therefore, I feel honored to be asked to write my story, as it may have limited relevance to others. I come from a rather dark background of having grown up in the 1960s in militaristic and intellectually dumbed-down San Diego. I was a bright, working-class kid who was fortunate to go to elementary and secondary private schools on scholarships. I am half Mexican. To most people, I look German or Polish. I am the only child from my parent's marriage, with three half-siblings who all died early in life. I never knew them.

When I told my father, whom my mother had already divorced, that I was going to transition, he told everyone that I had died. Begrudgingly, he came to accept me as his son, at the urging of his new spouse, prior to his death in 1996. Very recently, I found out from my mother, that my father actually had a family member who was a trans woman living in Mexico. She had been similarly ostracized by the family. After more than 30 years, post transition, my mother still does not fully accept me as her son. She is the only surviving member of my family of origin, or at least of the ones with whom I was allowed to have a relationship.

It may seem as if my life is filled mainly with trauma and tragedy, but I have also been the recipient of abundant fortune and many blessings. In

1974 I saw FTM pioneer, Jude Patton, on *The Phil Donohue Show* and wrote to him and made a connection that would become integral to my decision to transition. I already knew what a female-to-male transsexual was from reading Dr. Reuben's book, *All You Ever Wanted to Know about Sex but Were Afraid to Ask,* when I was 10 or 11-years-old, and understood that this was my issue. I was able to get this book through my best friend, whose mother worked for Dr. Reuben.

I was stunned as a 15 year-old when Jude, this man from the television talk show, responded to my letter almost immediately. He showed me a level of kindness and generosity that I had never experienced before. Jude lived in Orange County, in California about 90 minutes from my home, and I went to visit him as soon as I was old enough to drive. Jude played a key role in helping me to accept myself and his wonderfully supportive mother showed me that parents could be loving and supportive of their transsexual children. His Memorial Day parties introduced me to many other trans people, who were helpful and loving towards one another.

I tried to gain entrance to Stanford's Gender Identity program in 1977, when I turned 18 and was legally independent of my mother. It was over 500 miles away. I didn't have enough money for a hotel, so I drove all night and into the next day after working all day at a summer job. Unfortunately, I was rejected, and was told it was because of my youth and lack of family and social support. The latter was undeniably true. All my friends in school and in the neighborhood had rejected me when they learned of my plans to transition. But years later, I also learned that my mother had written a letter to the program urging them not to accept me. It was mailed before I ever had the evaluation. She told them that my high school girlfriend was behind my desire of "wanting to be a man."

In hindsight, it is interesting that I never questioned the procedure of how to gain entrance into this program. Part of growing up without civil rights, I suppose, can allow one to adopt the attitude akin to, "thank you for not killing me." I was so used to being victimized for being trans, that I thought that even people in a program like this would not necessarily treat me fairly. It is also in my "nature" to try and to try harder if obstacles are placed before me, rather than to devolve into self-destructive anger.

In 1979, a new gender program started in Orange County under the direction of William Heard, a psychologist. I was allowed to enter this program, I believe, because of Jude's support. Jude also introduced me to an 18-year-old transsexual man named John, who I quickly became close friends and lived with during the first few months of our transitions. He had already started hormones when I met him, and had been thrown out of his foster home at 18 when he disclosed his plans to transition.

In Dr. Heard's program I took my first injection of testosterone at 20 and had chest surgery a year later. I often took some flak from the older transsexuals in his therapy group for not working at a "real job" to save money for genital surgery. In my opinion, the mindset in those days was that in order to be "a man" and not a transsexual man, one needed to be invested in passing as much as possible. In this case, it involved having all the surgeries available and having them as quickly as possible.

I had always held part-time minimum-wage jobs while attending a university full time. I was driven by my underlying belief that I could not help being trans, but I did not want my whole life to revolve around this issue. I wanted to get an education so I could have a successful life apart from being trans, which I believed at the time would be a handicap. The rejection, lack of support, and abuse I received from my family and childhood friends concerning my transition clearly influenced my thinking. Therefore, I waited until I was almost finished with graduate school in clinical psychology in 1988 before pursuing more surgery. When I was ready to have the phalloplasty and hysterectomy surgeries, I moved to the Stanford area to do post-doctoral work so I would be near Dr. Donald Laub, the surgeon who had performed Jude's surgery. At the same time, I was attempting to complete my doctoral dissertation.

In 1988, I had a total hysterectomy, scrotoplasty, and a two-stage phalloplasty procedure known as the "suitcase handle" performed. Unfortunately, I lost the testicular expander, which was part of the scrotoplasty, to infection. I have yet to have *any* surgery, it seems, in which I do not acquire some sort of infection. This is due, in part, to the incredible amount of stress that I have lived in throughout my life and its impact on my immune system. The week prior to these surgeries, for example, I received my Ph.D. in psychology, which was quite an achievement since my parents never went to college and my father did not even complete high school. No one in my university or post-doc program knew of my transition, despite the fact that I had actually accomplished it between my sophomore and junior years in college and remained at the same university for graduate school. In hindsight, these accomplishments are all the more impressive given the utter lack of support from my family and not having any civil rights protection. It was also very stressful. I was often terrified of being "outed" and kicked out of the university. I was denied some opportunities to study abroad in graduate school, because I was unable to obtain a passport until completing genital surgery.

In 1997 I returned to Dr. Laub to attempt to have the urinary hook-up done and complete the scrotoplasty. I had electrolysis on my arm and scrotal area, the latter of which was the most painful procedure to date. Dr. Laub was able to extend the urethra through the clitoris and complete a vaginectomy but was unable to complete the hook-up. I had a strip of skin taken from my left arm to form the new urethra in my penis, and an artery to enhance feeling. The original tube of skin inside my penis, which had come from a hairy area under my naval, needed to be removed as it continued to cause problems. Nowadays, the hair is typically removed through electrolysis *prior* to any surgery being done.

I had developed feeling in my penis about a year post-surgery in 1989. My partner even said there was some enlargement and stiffening. To this day, I become angry when I read in articles and hear from physician presentations that phalloplasty leaves one with an "insensate organ"—that is, a flap of skin with no nerve sensation or feeling. I know, not only from my clinical training in sexual "dysfunction" but from my personal experience that the most powerful sex organ is between your ears. If you expect poor results, then this can influence what actually happens. When one relaxes, circulation can improve. If one feels ashamed or embarrassed by their body then it tends to withdraw. This can be a major issue in repeated erection concerns in non-transmen.

Shortly after my surgeries in 1997, Dr. Laub became ill and was forced to retire, which compelled me to see six different surgeons in my attempts to complete the urinary hook-up and scrotal implants. In 2010, I completed the first of what was to be a three-stage procedure with Dr. A in southern California, who was trying to complete what Dr. Laub originally started. Not only have these surgeries over the years been physically difficult but very frustrating, in that Dr. Laub did not write down what he was planning next, so none of the subsequent surgeons had a blueprint to draw on. Dr. A, who is board-certified in both urology and plastic surgery, has been the only physician willing to attempt surgery given these circumstances.

The primary reason Dr. Laub had not been able to complete the urinary hook-up during surgery in 1997 was that more hair needed to be removed than he had initially believed. Before proceeding further, I faced the daunting task of more extensive scrotal electrolysis. This time I planned to be anesthetized, even though I was concerned about the effect of more anesthesia on my long-term brain function. In February of 2011, I had the first stage of scrotal electrolysis and it took three months for me to fully recover cognitively from the anesthesia. I was easily distracted, and it was difficult for me to concentrate on more than one thing at a time. Even though, my initial agreement with the anesthesiologist, who worked in Dr. A's office, was that we would start with topical anesthesia and only proceed to a more whole body type, if this did not work, he started me on Versed and Propofol before I knew what was happening. When I saw Dr. A in the hallway prior to this procedure, he asked me if I thought he was insane to try this surgery. I was shocked by his question and responded that this was quite a question to ask of a psychologist.

These events convinced me to look for other options. As of the time of this writing, I am hopeful that a urologist who is completing a fellowship in plastic surgery might be able to assist me. He was introduced to me at the most recent World Professional Association for Transgender Health (WPATH), which I attended in part with hopes of meeting other surgeons. Dr. Laub's former patient coordinator introduced me to this physician, who apparently is in contact with Dr. Laub. I am keeping my fingers crossed.

There were also further bounties and blessings in my life. In 1995, under the auspices of learning more about urinary surgery, I attended the first FTM conference, held in San Francisco. Since then, I have come to befriend a number of wonderfully supportive trans people. In my role as a clinical psychologist, I have helped others in their journeys to transition and have been humbled to learn that many trans people have had a far worse time than I, in terms of finances, housing and social support. My partner and I have been married for over 21 years. I have a wide circle of friends and am more successful in my professional career than many of my non-transgender peers in psychology.

Earlier, I said my life has been one of trauma and tragedy and sadly, there were more tragedies to come. In 1986, my best friend, John, with whom I transitioned in the late 1970s, was murdered by the ex-husband of his girlfriend. During the murder trial in 1990, the defense proposed the argument that it was not a "real murder," as John was just an "it". The whole ordeal, which I followed in the newspapers, sent me into deep hiding with regard to being trans, as it also happened around the time I was licensed as a psychologist. I struggled then and for years afterwards with a belief that no matter what I did in terms of life success, when all was said and done, I would still just be a freak to the rest of the world, an "it" potentially worthy of justifiable homicide.

Life is what we make of it. As a dear friend told me last year, I could have become a hateful, hostile, and defeated person given my family background and the murder of my best friend. Instead, I have opted for a life of helping others and have even forgiven my friend's murderer, who has languished on death row since 1990. Over time, I have learned to accept with grace what I am given in life, whether it is good or bad. I believe being transgendered gives me a unique perspective on my non-trans clients' lives, which can help them break free from the rigidity of their more commonly held beliefs. Having multiple surgeries has given me a great deal of compassion to work with the physically disabled and with my elderly clients and their families. Being different sometimes can be a blessing rather than a curse. This is beautiful, poetic even.

The first 52 years of my life have been a long, strange trip, as Jerry Garcia of the Grateful Dead might have said. Even at this stage in my life, as I juggle a myriad of personal and professional projects from climbing the highest mountain in the 48 states to having a thriving private practice in Beverly Hills, I remember the mantra from my high school valedictorian speech, so many years ago: "You ain't seen nothing yet!" I believe it has always been my nature to believe the more I am pushed down the more I push on. Life is what one makes of it. Despite how negative or bleak things have seemed, I have usually been able to think of someone who is in worse shape or draw upon an inner strength with a ferocious Hispanic passion to say what one of my favorite film characters, Rocky Balboa, utters even after being knocked down in the ring, "I'm standing here. Take your best shot. Go for it"

I believe no one can stop you on your transitional journey when you believe in yourself. You can have a wonderful life. Embrace the positive and remember success in achieving your goals is the best revenge!

A Phoenix's Quest for the Dragon

Nickolas J. McDaniel

Stories about the phoenix have always inspired me. The phoenix is a mythical bird whose song has the ability to bring centeredness, contentment and happiness to those who hear it. The tears of the phoenix also have the ability to heal. When the phoenix reaches the end of its life cycle, it undergoes a kind of death, or more accurately, a rebirth through fire. The phoenix is reborn, rising from the ashes with even stronger healing properties of its song for the heart, and its tears for the flesh are stronger precisely because of its death by fire. For that reason, I have chosen the image of a blue phoenix entitled "A Peaceful Focus" as my logo. Like the phoenix I have undergone many "small deaths" only to be reborn stronger as a direct result of my experience. Gender Confirmation Surgery (GCS) was one of those transformative experiences.

Based upon my experiences and those shared with me by others, I think bottom surgery is most accurately described not as sex or genital reassignment surgery but as Gender Confirmation Surgery because that is what it does. For many it can further solidify and confirm one's identity in a spiritual and ceremonial way. As a result, the relationship I have not only with my body, but also with myself has improved, and my appearance reflects this. Since surgery, I have also been able to improve relationships with others because I can be truly authentic and have more intimate connections with friends and family.

My story may differ from that of other gender variant people because I never hid my gender identification as a boy and later as an adult man. Although society made assumptions based upon the anatomical configuration of my body, I never identified as female. My body lied but my heart knew the truth. Society saw it differently however, and I paid dearly for what others incorrectly deemed my gender transgression. As such, my experience and understanding of what it means to be trans differs from someone who resisted their own heart to conform to society. My personal pain resulted not from denying who I was, but rather from societal stigma. I constantly played the game of recognition politics. I wanted my identity as a man to be seen and respected by others, but instead it brought physical and verbal abuse from family, peers and complete strangers for three decades. In high school I was violently gang raped by seven or eight female classmates in my high school locker room to "teach it [me] to like being a female."

I have recognized and valued the malleability of gender since the age of two. I had no choice. I was born with a conflict between my mental gender identification and physical birth sex that forced this awareness. The vast majority of people have the luxury of never questioning gender, what it means, its potential fluidity, or how their own gender identity fits into the mix. For many cis-gendered people, questioning that which they have always seen as unalterable is uncomfortable, and understandably so. Being born gender/sex congruent is a luxury, and in contemporary American society, a privilege. Normatively gendered people think gender is some concrete thing that cannot be altered. However, as with anything that involves social construction, what it means to be a man, woman or the gender roles attributed to male-bodied or female-bodied people, varies from one culture and generation to the next. A gender role or presentation socially ascribed to a masculine or feminine body and considered appropriate in one cultural space or time can easily be considered inappropriate in another.

Those of us who do dare to question our own maleness or femaleness are perceived as a threat because we question the traditionally accepted gender binary, and by virtue of our own existence, force cis-gendered people to question not only their gender but everything they were taught about gender. Rather than question their own gender and beliefs and adopting a more accurate view of gender as a universe of infinite possibilities, however, the majority thrusts the responsibility of their own discomfort onto trans people to "prove" our own existence, validity, and worth. For the transitioning individual, they must not only struggle with societal reaction by "proving" their own maleness or femaleness, but also define what it means to be a man, woman or another gender while also undergoing a major physical and mental transition. That is no small feat!

The dissonance between the lie my body told and the truth in my heart was so extreme that from the age of six, suicide seemed like the only friend I had. I spent the better part of ten years misdiagnosed, overmedicated, and incorrectly treated to "cure" my "mental defect." In reality, it was my body that was defective and society used it to marginalize me. At an early age I understood that bodies could lie but hearts don't. I grew up in a conservative bedroom community in central California where I rarely encountered images of transwomen and none of transmen. Seeing the movie *Boys Don't Cry* in 1999 at an indie theater was literally a life-saving experience. For the first time, I saw someone with whom I could identify and learned the language to begin expressing what was going on with me in a way that someone could understand. I finally knew what I needed. I followed the Harry Benjamin Standards of Care and utilized hormone therapy, and then fought my medical insurance provider and won coverage for top surgery, which was completed in January 2003.

I knew little about phalloplasty when I flew to the Midwest for a surgery consultation in August 2005. It wasn't for lack of trying. As soon as I began my physical transition, I had also begun researching bottom surgery. Very little information existed about GCS for female-bodied men at the time. Most of the available information concentrated on vaginoplasty and labiaplasty for transwomen. The majority of resources about GCS for female-bodied men concentrated on metoidioplasty with a brief mention of phalloplasty, and usually concentrated on old, outdated procedures and results.

I asked other transmasculine people about phalloplasty, and quickly became acquainted with "anti-phallo sentiment" in the community, which often seemed based on judgments, opinions and outdated information rather than facts. Researching my surgical options was difficult and frustrating. When I asked one prominent American GCS surgeon about phalloplasty he replied, "It's an outdated surgery that no one wants anymore." But this was not true. Since beginning my surgery, I have been contacted by many transmen researching their options to ask about my experience. Like me, they are looking for factual information to make informed decisions for themselves.

The consultation helped me choose the right surgeon, and I have not regretted my choice. I knew without question that the only procedure for me was phalloplasty so I followed my heart. I knew that metoidioplasty would not erase enough of the lie "down there" to ease the discomfort I felt and allow me to get on with my life. So I didn't even consider it.

Since 2005 I have had seven major surgeries performed in hospitals and at least 16 more procedures performed in the surgeon's office. My surgery was experimental, as the donor skin was taken from an atypical location, the abdominal panniculus. So far I've been working on this for almost six years now and still have no ability to void or have an erection yet. At present, the dragon still sleeps. After the next stage (which will give me the ability to function) I will have spent in excess of $100,000. And no, I still won't be done: at least not quite yet. But wow, I can honestly say so far I have a beautiful Ferrari in the garage and cannot wait for the day I can take it out for a spin, drop some jaws, and turn some heads. It may not be perfect, but at least it exists and is a work in progress. Until then all I can do is stand in the garage, look, drool, and dream. It is an image that inspires some impressive dreams.

Phalloplasty should not be taken lightly. The process will test even the strongest of hearts in many ways. I can honestly say that phalloplasty has been one of the hardest things I have ever done. To date it has tested me mentally, emotionally, physically and financially. It's something that one must be hungry and starving to death for. While my ability to say "yes" to sex for the first time in my life will be nice someday, sex had little to do with my need for phalloplasty. I was fueled by the need to be fully comfortable in my own skin for the first time.

In addition to the poor and pithy information on phalloplasty, I faced other challenges and struggles in my quest. My older brother had been my biggest cheerleader from day one until I announced my intention for phalloplasty. Then he said, "You were happy with what you had." Uh, no. I was still showering and dressing in the dark, unable to face seeing the lie that my body told and melting down privately when I was forced to confront the reality. I felt tortured by my body. Although I wanted to date, I could not even consider doing anything below the belt. Suicide, though no longer the focus of my life, was still something I considered occasionally because of my emotional pain.

My gender specialist told me that only seven percent of brothers of transmen come back to the sibling relationship. The trans brother's transition repositions the cis-gender brother's place in the family, which can create tension in their relationship. The cis-gendered sibling needs to find his new position in the family, as it becomes clear that he is no longer the only son. And then there's penis size, which can enhance the tension, since size is a big deal for many men. The first question a surgeon asks is, "How big do you want to be?" What if by some chance the cis-gendered sibling notices that his penis is smaller than his trans brother's penis?

In the end I was extremely fortunate. Relations with my brother were awkward for about a year, but eventually he came around and asked me to be one of the groomsmen at his wedding. Now we are close once again. Not a day goes by that I am not deeply grateful to have my brother back in my life. Sadly, I know that everyone it not as fortunate.

Going to get transition-related surgeries is a highly emotional experience and emotional and social support is critical. I had assumed that the bulk of my support would come from gender variant peers who could relate to me because of their own experiences. Not always. With my initial surgery, support from gender variant peers was overwhelming and touching. As the surgeries dragged on over months, then years, however, their support gradually waned into a quiet, tired exasperation, which I could understand, because, at times, it mirrored my own feelings. When announcing another return to the Midwest for surgery, I heard, "Again?! When will it *finally* be over?" I couldn't answer that question for myself, much less for others. It *had* been a long time. Many times I wished that I knew someone who had been through surgery before me to discuss things with.

Phalloplasty has tested me. Yet, just as in other parts of my transition, I find that these challenges are like being reborn from the fire. I am emerging stronger than I could have ever imagined. Making my body a home where I can live peacefully has without a doubt been the best investment in myself I have ever (or probably ever will) make in myself. My truth is that I don't identify as transsexual, transman, FTM, transmasculine, etc. (though I do respect those who do). For me, being born female-bodied was a birth defect that I corrected with medical assistance. It is no more who I am than my brain tumor, flu, allergies or bronchitis. Although the process of surviving it and then undergoing transition has helped shape the man I am (and more than just physically). I can truly say without guilt or shame for the first time in my life that I love who I am and feel able to embrace life.

Since embarking on this transformation journey, I have dedicated my life to making this world a better place. I do what I can to prevent others from being dehumanized like I was. I work in the trans community as a professional and serve as a support resource for other female-bodied men, FTMs, transmen, and masculine-spectrum folks. I am a gender specialist and sex therapy intern and work with gender dysphoric individuals to support and help guide them as they embark on their own transitioning adventure and write their own gender maps. My purpose is to help others to feel better about themselves and the skin in which they live. I embrace every opportunity to educate others about gender variance in the hopes of combating transphobia. My song now rings proud, confident and true precisely because I have been tested, both by societal stigma in my formative years and by the process of physical transition and phalloplasty.

Phalloplasty has also liberated me from dysphoric feelings and allowed me to begin dating for the first time in my life. This presents its own challenge in and of itself complicated by my history of both gender variance and childhood sexual abuse. My approach is to let a date get the opportunity to know me for a while and see what the chemistry is like between us before I have "The Talk." You know, the one that starts, "There's something you should know." I haven't had much luck so far. However, everyone experiences rejection for a myriad of reasons no matter what their gender history. It makes finding that special someone truly magical.

Prior to surgery, I was warned about "phantom pain" and that I might experience discomfort due to the weight of new anatomy hanging in front of me. However, just as with top surgery my experience was completely opposite. I will never forget the first time I walked up a hill after scrotoplasty at the University of California in Santa Cruz, I could feel the difference. I realized in that moment that I'd had phantom pain *before* surgery, not after. Things now felt *right*. For the first time, my body was no longer a body bag that I was trapped in and desperate to escape at all costs. I knew in that moment that I was on the way to finally feeling at home in my body. The sense of relief was huge.

Although progress in phalloplasty in the past five years has been impressive, I know that no amount of surgery will give me what I should have been born with, or fully correct the lie my body once told. I know I will never be able to be a biological parent. I also know the measure of a man (or a woman or pangendered individual) is not the size or function of their genitals, but rather the goodness of their heart and actions. In that regard, I now know I am more man than many males who had the privilege of being born gender-congruent.

At the time of this writing, my physical transformation is not yet complete. My genitals have a certain anatomical untruthfulness in their ambiguity. While they are not standard male plumbing, more importantly they bear no resemblance to female genitalia. My genitals tell their own transitioning truth. Yet, their newfound ability via a pair of helping surgical hands to tell the truth of my gender has also freed me to tell my own truth. I know what a luxury it is to have access to this cutting-edge technology, and a day doesn't go by that I do not feel deeply grateful. I wish it were an option available to anyone who wants it. My complaints overall are few and improvements are welcomed.

My truth is whom you see before you: a man who has just given you the gift of insight into his struggle to correct his birth defect through phalloplasty in the hopes that it can in some way help ease another man's journey. It is upon the wings of my heart that I now soar higher than I ever could have dreamed because after six years, the phoenix has ended his quest to find the dragon. Now, it is just a matter of getting the sleeping dragon to awake, rise and leave the garage!

Phalloplasty Fallacies

David E. Weekley

I transitioned nearly four decades ago, and I chose for years to live my life quietly as a white, heterosexual male for many reasons. Opinions in our community vary about whether one "should" only live openly as a trans-sexual person or have the freedom to simply live quietly in society experiencing the fullness of who we are. This is a personal choice, as are the decisions regarding bottom surgery or any surgery. For me there was never a question about whether I would share my personal history; it was always a matter of when. At the time I transitioned the shared belief according to *The Harry Benjamin Standards of Care* was for transgender people to create a new history, only sharing their real story if absolutely necessary. I hoped my experience living in our culture as a white, heterosexual male would someday help my life as an activist and advocate for inclusivity.

As a person of faith, I sought God's perfect timing for this moment. As a clergyman, it was my hope to make a difference in how people of faith viewed transsexual people by serving congregations quietly and later revealing my full story and identity as a transsexual man. In religious language for some people, God's timing is referred to as *kairos*. I always knew this time would come, and come it did. Nearly three years ago I shared my story and history as a transsexual man with my congregation, colleagues and the world. While I had worked for inclusivity and TLGBQ (transgender, lesbian, gay, bisexual, and queer/questioning) rights for years, I now needed to speak my own truth. This announcement resituated me publically in the gender non-conforming world. As I became acquainted with the TLGBQ community, I was dismayed of how some people talked about and treated one another. This extended to discussions about FTM bottom surgery where people made hypercritical and judgmental remarks about genital surgery and men who had them. None of these people spoke from experiences of having surgery, and many did not even identify as trans, male, or masculine.

At the time I went through my transition from a biologically-defined female to male, few options were available about how things would progress. I had little or no control over whether I was termed an "acceptable candidate" for sex reassignment surgery. As a 21 year old desperate young man who truly did feel trapped in the wrong body, I did not understand all that was going on in the medical, psychological, and social world in which I lived. I only knew that I wanted and needed to become the man I knew myself to be.

One component of my wholeness was phalloplasty surgery. It was a significant component of expressing myself and connecting with my female partners as a lover, and as a human being whose expression of sexuality came in the form of a male gender identity. At the time I transitioned, this was viewed as an integral part of transitioning, so it was never an issue with the medical team involved in my care. In fact, my *initial* surgery was the phalloplasty. This surgery preceded the others because the procedure was the most complicated, delicate, and extensive part of my medical transition. As I read about this surgery I discovered phalloplasty was initially developed to help repair genital injuries among men serving in the military. It was known to be risky and, in fact, it did not always work. Sometimes the graft did not take, or other post-surgical complications could develop. I was aware of this history at the time, but I knew that I was willing to undergo this procedure to complete my transition and achieve a sense of wholeness I had never known.

Once deemed an "acceptable candidate," I followed the required steps leading to this surgical procedure. I lived fully as a man for one year, during which time I established employment, and changed my sex on all the legal documents that I was able to prior to surgery. I entered the hospital in November of 1974. I was frightened, but never reluctant. Phalloplasty was the completion of myself as a human being. I strongly desired to please my lover, a heterosexual young woman, and to be the whole man I knew myself to be.

I experienced no question and no struggle inside myself regarding this aspect of my identity.

Contrary to what I hear from some critics of phalloplasty today, this was never a matter of power, nor an issue about which biological sex was the "best". I was not trying to gain "white male privilege" by having surgery. I simply wanted to be myself and this was one essential aspect of that goal. To this day, I remain grateful to the capable surgeons and the medical team who welcomed me as a transsexual man and helped me through those complex years. It may be difficult, if not impossible, for people transitioning today to appreciate this history and the courage required by both the medical teams and the transpeople involved at such a pioneering time.

While much has improved in the process of transitioning, and in the medical procedures involved, the degree of contention surrounding personal choices about how, why, and when a person transitions distresses me. I am shocked at the debates and the too often judgmental opinions about transmen who pursue "bottom surgery." When I transitioned, it was a given that phalloplasty was the initial step in a full medical transition to male. While I believe it is good that people have options, at the same time I am dismayed by the amount of arguing and dissention, especially among those who identify as trans-masculine, regarding whether, or which type of bottom surgery is best. Too often the most judgmental comments come from those who have never opted for this type of surgery. I firmly believe people should not, speak about an experience of which they know nothing about personally.

Today bottom surgery means either the construction of a functional penis, or other types of genital reconstruction surgery, such as metoidioplasty, to help transmen become the person they desire to express in daily life. I do not comprehend the judgment, debate, and hostility directed at those of us who fulfill our male gender identity through such surgeries. Some personal acquaintances have said that their negative comments are based on fear of surgery or an inability to cover the costs. I do understand that, for some, phalloplasty is not something they are personally choosing at this time, which is fine, but they do not, should not, and cannot speak for those of us who have made the decision to embrace a dimension of maleness that, for many, completes us as men. Why not, "live and let live" and respect our different decisions?

As for the costs of surgery, I was fortunate at the time I transitioned that my insurance covered much of my medical expenses. Still, I had to work, sometimes holding down two jobs, to help pay the remaining costs and my living expenses. Since surgery, I have worked and advocated for change in health policies that exclude trans people from coverage. Fortunately, some insurance programs and companies are again covering some of these procedures.

Sometimes I wonder if the attitudes of some lesbian feminists contribute to the problematic dialogue about bottom surgery. I have read some feminist essays and books that deny and denigrate transmen and assume that transitioning is a rejection of femaleness and desire for "male privilege."[1] As someone who has lived socially as a white male for more than three decades I find this is a false line of reasoning. My motivation was purely survival. I had to be who I am and surgery was the only way I could embrace the fullness of life rather than death, which can take many forms, including, literally dying.

In contemporary American culture, the amount of anger I have seen exhibited towards men in general does not make life easy for transsexual men. Historically, transwomen have had and continue to have significant difficulties with acceptance by cis-gender feminists. In my personal experience, moreover, I witness some cis-gender feminists extending even less compassion to transmen. The assumption is that we are embracing the power differences of the patriarchal system, when my lived experience and politics could not be further from this position of inequality. Having been raised and socialized as female I genuinely understand the horrendous abuse and inequality women bear.

Functioning as a man in contemporary culture, I hear the remarks made by those cis-gender men who continue to buy into an abusive and unequal patriarchal ideology and value system. But I do not subscribe to it and work to change this unhealthy dimension of society in every way and by every means possible. This means I do not fit into the dominant patriarchal system either, and so I am often left on the "outside" both by gender conforming groups and the TLGBQ community. This can be a lonely place, as many other transsexual men testify. It is deeply disheartening and hurtful to be dismissed by those who assail transsexual men in this way.

Despite the negative comments made by some regarding bottom surgery, I still remain satisfied and pleased with my surgery. I understood from the outset that there would be differences in how I would function compared with cis-gender males. It took me time to work through some of the ups and downs (no pun intended), but I never doubted that I wanted this procedure. Some good aspects of being different from cis-gender males are that I have never had to worry about size, premature ejaculation, unplanned pregnancies, or erectile dysfunction. I experienced no medical problems, and I continue to enjoy my intimate relationship with my spouse. All in all, I continue to function as a happy male.

Many more surgical options are available now. I did not have the same choices. But, if given the same information and opportunities today, I would still choose the same surgery I underwent over three decades ago. Some things I hear on social networks are utterly ridiculous. My penis does not look like a "carrot" nor is my partner unsatisfied when we make love. Like many couples we embrace a variety of techniques for creative love-making, and, for us, it is all good.

As I read or listen to debates about any transition surgery, I believe the most important question those of us who identify as transmen must ask for ourselves is: what does it mean to be a man? This is a personal journey of self-discovery, and one that can be undertaken by consultation with physicians, counselors, and talking with other transsexual men who have already gone through this process. Whatever decision one makes about bottom surgery, it requires courage and commitment. I respect the decisions others make regarding phalloplasty, or any other type of reassignment surgery. Rather than arguing amongst ourselves and either embracing or negating bottom surgery, and subsequently negating the value of those who make choices different from our own, the better path might be to join together, share information and experiences, and encourage one another. No matter our gender identification, as transgender human beings we live in a unique space and place in our culture. If we can refrain from placing labels and making value-judgments about each other and our personal choices and decisions, we may actually help create something unique. We all lose when we attempt to make others conform to our personal choices. We all win when we support individual freedom.

Endnotes

1 For examples, see Sheila Jeffries, *Unpacking Queer Politics: A Lesbian Feminist Perspective*, (Cambridge, UK: Polity Press, 2003), and the following blogs: http://dirtywhiteboi67.blogspot.com/ and http://factcheckme.wordpress.com/2012/07/08/on-gay-transmen/.

All It Takes is Time and Tramadol

John Henry

My priorities changed over the course of transitioning. The first goal was to reconstruct my chest, which was the most distressing. But bottom surgery was different. People who passed me in the street could not tell the difference between my packer and the real thing, but I knew and I could not hide from myself or my feelings. I never thought that I would ever have a fully functioning penis. It seemed so far out of reach. I did not have the money to go private, and the National Health Service (NHS) in England would not even pay for my mastectomy. So phalloplasty was definitely out of the picture or so I believed at the time. Television documentaries and the few people I had spoken with had given me the impression that the surgery would allow me to either have an erection or stand and pee, but not both. Still I wanted both.

The surgical results that I had seen were not promising. I was not sure if I wanted to go through all that surgery for something that looked only remotely like a penis and, if I was lucky, would not leak when I tried to pee. It was also incredibly expensive and involved a lot of time taken off from work. No one knew about my past, and I intended for it to stay that way. So I put the idea of bottom surgery back in the corner of my mind and made the most of what I had. Then I got married and things changed.

Marriage changed the way I viewed myself and although my wife never wanted me to have any type of surgery because of the risks involved, I felt inadequate and could not be the husband that I wanted to be. She said that she had never seen me as anything other than a man and that the decision was ultimately mine and she would support me in whatever I decided. Despite her support, however, I never made any serious inquiries into bottom surgery until my marriage broke down. Afterwards, I became more aware of what I wanted and decided to do it for myself, but I still did not know what kinds of surgeries were available. I wanted to be able to pee standing up and have an erection. I also wanted to have a convincing looking penis that would not draw attention in the showers and did not look like I had been savaged by a dog. I did not think that was too much to ask.

My endocrinologist referred me for further bottom surgery and said that I also needed referrals from two psychiatrists at the Gender Identity Clinic in London. The psychiatrists asked me the usual basic questions, explained the types of surgery available, and asked about my support system. My wife was there, but I did not mention our separation in part because I thought that it could only slow down the process. The last thing I wanted was a trip to a marriage therapist before I could get referred. I did not deliberately deceive my doctors as much as I was fooling myself. I had hoped that my wife and I would get back together, which eventually happened, but, at the time, she had other plans. I later came to realize just how important a good support network is when going through this journey—not just emotionally but physically. It is necessary to rest in order to recover and heal, and, although it is possible to butter toast with one hand and wash without standing up, it is much easier if someone is there to help with these things.

Several different methods offered the kind of bulge in my trousers that I wanted and I had narrowed it down to two. I thought the radial forearm phalloplasty gave the best visual results and added the bonus of sensation. Some people could achieve orgasm from this surgery. The big drawback of this procedure was the scar left on the forearm. I would have to conceal those scars from colleagues, so I thought that the pubic phalloplasty procedure would be better for me. Many could see my arm but few would see what was underneath my clothes and in my trousers. I also had to consider how much time I would need to take off from work and how I would cope when returning, because I have a physically demanding job. The radial forearm operation would be less traumatic on the stomach, but overall I believed the pubic phalloplasty would be easier to conceal and pass off as something else. I chose to tell people I had a hernia and needed abdominal surgery. I was granted six to eight weeks of recovery time and light duties upon returning to work, which suited my needs perfectly.

Things moved on quickly, and I was referred to Dr. Nim Christopher at Saint Peter's Andrology Centre in London. I was surprised by the many phalloplasty options available and even more that all the costs were covered by the NHS. I only had to pay the train fare to London. My doctor was laid back and confident in his ability to deal with any potential problems. It seemed he assumed that I knew more about the procedures than was really the case. I was not prepared for things to be so straight forward and so did not ask the questions I probably should have. I discovered later that I should have asked more questions about the details of the surgery and recovery. Perhaps he thought I knew more than I did or did not think they were important at the time. When my doctor told me how long I would need to stay off work after each stage of surgery, he made it sound simple. Each of the two big operations would require six weeks off work to recover, while the three smaller operations would each require a week off. This sounded great. I planned to do the first two surgeries using sick-leave and the rest using holidays. Unfortunately, as I later discovered, those recovery times were ambitious and overly optimistic, as I needed much more time to recover. Either, I did not recover as fast as his previous patients or I was not fully informed about recovery details. The doctor failed to mention the many trips needed to my local clinic for changing dressings and removing stitches for which I needed to make convincing excuses to leave work twice a week. The check-ups located at Harley Street in the South of England were a long trip for me since I was traveling from the North. It was not a quick stop. The trip required planning and time.

My doctor told me I would be able to obtain an erection and pee standing up following surgery. To do so, they needed to take a vein and small piece of skin from my forearm to make my urethra. They said it would only be a small scar on my arm, which I could easily come up with a plausible excuse at work to tell the lads. I did not expect a whopping bloody big scar that runs from my wrist to my elbow. The scar around my waist also runs almost completely around my body. I then questioned whether I had made the right decision, but it was too late to dwell on that now. I look at pictures of some of the worse scars left after radial arm phalloplasty and think if that was me, I would have regretted choosing that method also. Overall, I think I made the best decision possible at the time. The only regret I have is not speaking with other men who had already been through the process and seeing their results. I think that might have helped me make a more informed decision and be better prepared for what was to follow in the ensuing months and years.

My surgery was performed at the Hospital of Saint John and Saint Elizabeth in Saint John's Wood, London. I had a private room with cable television, phone and waiter service. The food was fantastic, and they even served afternoon tea and cake. I was always on the same ward and with the same nursing team, and they became like a family to me, especially since I had no visitors. I cannot praise them highly enough. It was better than being on holiday.

Another detail I wasn't told was the enema they gave me the night before the first operation, and looking back, I'm glad because I would have stressed about it. I was chilled out on my bed watching television—when the nurse came in, removed my pants and scuttled me off to the bathroom. It was not the best way to start my first night but it was over before I knew it. Once they finished fiddling with me, checking my blood pressure, filling out forms, and taking blood, they left me alone. I tend to take things in stride as they come and this was something that I wanted so I did not worry obsessively. The next thing I knew, I was in a recovery room with a gorgeous nurse smiling down at me and soon after that, I was back in my room. I couldn't move and didn't want to. The pain was incredible. I was on self-administered morphine and when I lay still it was fine, sometimes uncomfortable but bearable. But when the nurses tried to move me, I was in total agony.

Next to turn up was my torturer, the physical therapist. At first, she got me pumping my arms and wiggling my feet, which helped keep my circulation going and increased my heart rate and breathing to help keep my lungs clear. It also made me look like I had a screw loose. I never realized resting could be so bad for me. Then a few days later she got me on my feet, shuffling around the ward with my bag of pee in a carrier bag! At this point I was still catheterized. I saw a couple of different physical therapists while I was recovering and they were (nearly) all gorgeous. What a bonus!

I was discharged at the end of the week and told to take Paracetamol as needed. I had been on morphine in the hospital but was sent home without pain medication. After waiting at Euston for a ticket, then a packet of

Paracetamol, a bottle of water, and finally missing my train literally by seconds because I couldn't walk fast enough, I made sure to pack some painkillers for subsequent operations.

The pain and discomfort I endured the first few weeks after coming home was unbearable at times. I would lie in bed wondering, *what the hell was I doing?* I could not lie down flat, but sitting up also caused pain in my back and shoulders. The unbearable pain made me want to cry at times. I remember watching Julie Andrews in *Victor, Victoria* when I was younger and vowing that I would rather die than to go through that sort of pain, isolation and desperation. But here I was, alone and in excruciating pain, questioning myself and my judgment. It is these times we need someone close to help us through emotionally. Things improved as I healed, and in time, I forgot about the pain and began to plan for the next stage of phalloplasty.

I was told that for phalloplasty surgeons initially craft larger penises than necessary in case some length is lost due to complications. My surgeon attempted to slim mine down in the last operation. It is fine in the middle but looks a little like Captain Caveman's club because the tip is a little larger than the shaft. More work is needed to taper it better.

Like the surgeon and other staff at Saint Peter's, the next team in the hospital seemed to assume I already knew the procedures to be performed. Once again, I did not ask questions but simply placed myself in their hands. I should have asked more questions. The staff was approachable, and I found Mandi, one of the nurses from Saint Peters, helpful with problems I had while recovering at home. At times, I wondered if the pain would ever stop or if something had gone wrong. When I emailed the district nurses, they reminded me of everything I had gone through. The psychiatrist at the clinic told me not to worry because the pain would go away in time, which lessened my anxiety.

I didn't know until leaving that the district nurses would be coming to my home to check my dressings and remove the stitches. I had heard stories of nurses ridiculing trans patients out of ignorance of our condition. Looking back, it was quite obvious that I wouldn't be able to get out to the clinic on my own, but I never thought about what the alternative would be. I was dreading the experience, but my fears of mistreatment did not pan out. In fact, the nurse who initially looked after me, Helen, was magnificent. She still stops for a chat when we meet in public, and she is always interested in how I am doing. I was, and still am, a novelty for the district nursing team. They would fight over who was going to cover me, as they the found me more interesting than their other patients.

The way I feel about myself and in my body, even my confidence levels, changed from one operation to the next. The initial operation changed the way I felt about myself. Throwing the packer in the trash bin was great. I got an enormous burst of self-confidence knowing that the bulge in my trousers was all me. It was also reassuring to know that nothing was going to fall out of my pants. I went from being someone who was totally ashamed of my body to someone who can easily strip off in the showers now after swimming. The fact that half of the NHS has seen my tackle could also have something to do with losing my inhibitions.

In the second stage, the surgeon created the urethra in my shaft from that "small" piece of skin from my arm. I was in for one hell of a shock when the nurse undressed my penis after a week. The hole at the other end was a shock too. The surgical team didn't describe in any detail what they were going to do around the clitoris, so it was another shock to find a hole at the side of it and part of the 'hood' all hard and stitched up. Eventually, it all became clear what they were doing. But at the time I wondered if I would ever get any pleasure from it again. The weirdest part was cleaning out the new tube with a syringe of warm water daily. It was like peeing backwards.

In the third operation they hooked up my urethra. I had a catheter in for a while after surgery to allow the new tube to heal. It was strange not to go to the toilet, but I soon got used to it. When it was time for the catheter to come out, the nurse capped off the end, removed the bag, and gave me the best advice I've ever heard from a nurse: "Go to the pub for a couple of pints and don't come back until you've peed twice." I expected it to take some time getting used to standing and peeing but it didn't feel weird at all. It felt right. That was a bit of a let-down in a way, because I thought that I would be ecstatic. But I wasn't. It just felt "normal" and more of a relief than anything. I am not anxious about using public toilets anymore if there's no cubicle. I can use urinals in the gents instead of waiting for a cubicle which makes it less stressful if I go out with the lads after work for a drink or to a rugby game or concert. My only problem is that I've got short legs and sometimes when the bowl is too high I can't reach it. I have had to pee on my tip-toes occasionally. The main problem at first was getting used to "milking" my penis. The urine doesn't just drain all the way out like in a natural penis so I have to help it along with a gentle squeeze starting at the base. If I don't do this a few drops of urine will remain in the shaft and leak out into my shorts. I carried a spare pair of underwear for the first few weeks until I got used to it.

I've had four of the five operations needed to complete this process, which has taken two years so far. The fifth surgery could have been completed by now, but my work commitments have not allowed so. Also, the longer I wait between stages the better because my body can heal more before the next slicing and dicing begins. I had already waited 36 years for my penis so I am in no hurry. Moreover, each time I underwent surgery I had to lie to my boss to get time off, which meant that I could not afford for anything to go wrong. So taking things slowly up to now has gone well.

It has not all been positive. I had bouts of depression, mostly because I felt so alone. No one came to visit me in the hospital. No one came to take me home. My second operation was particularly bad. My left arm was in a sling, my right arm was hooked up to a drip, I had morphine in a drip, and my legs were in special inflatable socks to prevent blood clots from forming. I couldn't move and had to stay that way for at least three days. My blood pressure was very low and I was drifting in and out of sleep much of the time. I woke up one night to find the night nurse sitting with me. She stayed with me, pushing fluids into me, making sure I made it through the night in one piece. She knew I wasn't expecting visitors so the next night she brought some cream and massaged my shoulders, back and bottom so I didn't get too sore from lying so still. She did this every night for a week. I will never forget her. This nurse was a true angel.

My surgeon and I had different opinions about penis size. He seemed surprised when I told him my penis was too fat. I don't know what reactions he's had from previous patients but I wanted a penis that wouldn't make me look deformed. I wanted the penis I had envisioned before surgery. I had not gone through all that pain to end up with something different. Although my wife and I were separated at the time, we still discussed what would be a practical girth. He trimmed it down twice and although the base is still relatively fat, it is more functional for intercourse. My wife and I are now back together, and I am glad that we discussed the matter and that I did not just allow the surgeon to create his ideal.

Before rekindling things with my wife, I did not have the confidence to date women as I was very aware of being different and I never knew how they'd react. I've never felt like I fit in anywhere, and I'm still searching for a place that I can be myself. The trans community offers that to a certain degree but work and personal commitments prevent me from taking part in many of the activities that could help me feel more part of the community. I was hoping that surgery would make me feel more like the men I work with. Instead, it has actually made me more aware of how different I am from them. I couldn't relate to physical sensations men were talking about as I wasn't capable of those sensations. I feel somewhat isolated, which is the last thing I ever thought that transitioning would do. Having my wife back has helped me feel more settled and secure, but I am still aware of the differences between myself and biological males. I think before any surgery, when I was binding my chest and using a packer, I had the idea that surgery would correct all the problems I'd faced growing up. Once I'd had the surgery, however, the realization hit me that no matter how good the surgeon was or how many operations I had, not only will I not be the same as a biological male but I will also no longer have the body I once had. I was now somewhere completely new, different from anywhere I had known.

As I could now use male urinals I became aware of the possibility of the man standing next to me being able to see my penis. Would he see the scar and if so would he freak out? Even though my penis is now thinned, it is still bigger than most flaccid penises, which could draw attention in a public toilet should it be noticed. I suppose I was kidding myself that surgery would make me the man I've always known I am. It has failed to live up to that ideal. Phalloplasty has provided me with the tools to forge a different life to the one I had lived for many years, but I will always be different and that is something I am more aware of now than ever before. Sometimes, I feel bitter that I and others like me have to go through all this pain and suffering just to be ourselves. I am jealous of bio men who don't realize how lucky they are to be biologically and anatomically male from birth. But then I also realize how fortunate I am to have the opportunity to have these operations. Many people never make it this far. What I've gone through and am still going through has made me realize how strong I am. I have met some incredible and unforgettable people on this journey.

The emotional rollercoaster that I continue experiencing is incredible. There have been times when the pain was unbearable that I have questioned what I have done. But with time and Tramadol (pain medication), I have gotten through it. While my wife has been supportive, I have nonetheless felt alone throughout this process. For other men, I recommend having a support network through this arduous process.

What I do have is a brilliant general practitioner who empathizes and supports me every step of the way. If you work for a company that requires doctors' reports for everything, you will want a doctor who knows how to be honest yet vague in the reports. I'm looking forward to the last surgery, completing the surgical process, and finally being able to have intercourse. My wife once said that I am the only person she has ever met who got their virginity back.

The First Man-Made Man[1]

Pagan Kennedy

Michael Dillon, a bearded medical student, fiddled with his pipe and then lit it nervously. The year was 1950.... the word *transsexual* had yet to enter common usage. Almost no medical literature acknowledged that thousands of people felt *trapped in the wrong body* and would do anything—including risk death—to change their sex. Michael Dillon, [a] medical student, had authored what was then one of the few books in the world to delve into the subject. In an eccentric little volume called *Self: A Study in Ethics and Endocrinology (1946)*, he had argued on behalf of [transsexual] people.... Dillon proposed an idea that seemed wildly radical at the time: why not give patients the body they wanted? Thanks to recent technological breakthroughs, doctors could transform a man into a woman and vice versa. But because of the stigma against these sex changes—as well as laws that prohibited castration—only a few people in the world had ever crossed the line...

More than a decade earlier, an athletic blonde named Laura Dillon roared through the streets of Bristol on her motorbike. She wore her hair short, and a sports jacket hid her breasts; a skirt, her only concession to femininity, flapped around her calves. With her broad shoulders, patrician accent, and Eton haircut, she could easily pass for a pampered young man.... At first glance, Laura seemed to be a fellow just out of Oxford, dismounting his motorbike with a dashing leap. But blink again and Laura was nothing but a cross-dressed girl. People who passed her on the street couldn't help staring, confused by the double image she presented.... She knew herself to be a man, a man who was disappearing inside a ridiculous body, underneath breasts and hips. She didn't think she could go on this way anymore.

Pills saved her. Laura Dillon had managed to get hold of testosterone pills in 1938, soon after she'd graduated from college. She became the first woman on record to take the drug with the intention of changing her sex. Over several years, the hormone therapy transformed her into a muscular, deep-voiced man with fuzz on his cheeks. As soon as Dillon could look entirely male, he became invisible. Pumping petrol at the garage where he worked, greasy in his coveralls, Dillon easily passed as just another workingman. More than passed. He became bland-looking, unremarkable, ordinary—which was what he'd always wanted. He could stroll down the street now, could step into a hardware store or a men's bathroom, without attracting the least bit of attention. By the early 1940s, Dillon had mustered the courage to leave the garage for medical school—under his male name.

But hormones could only take Dillon so far. If other men caught a glimpse of him in the locker room or public baths, they would immediately know he had been born female. So in the early 1940s, Dillon sought out Sir Harold Gillies, Britain's top plastic surgeon. Gillies had reconstructed the genitals of soldiers who'd been bombed or burned, but he had never built a penis from scratch on a woman's body. It would be grueling, and Gillies could not guarantee the results. At least the operation would be legal. While an arcane law protected male genitals from "mutilation", no such bans applied to female genitals and reproductive organs.

Dillon would eventually undergo a series of 13 operations to construct a penis. He began the treatments in 1946, while he was a student at Trinity College medical school in Dublin, and he finished his surgeries in 1949. Gillies had to harvest skin for the new organ from Dillon's legs and stomach; Dillon suffered from oozing infections where the skin had been flayed; at times, he was so debilitated he had to walk with a cane. And why did Dillon want the penis so badly? Not necessarily for sex. Rather, a penis would serve as a membership card into the world of men, their bathrooms, their rowing teams, and their gentlemen's clubs in London. The lack of a penis had held him back, "for without some form of external organ he could hardly undress for the shower with the rest of the crew," as Gillies noted. Furthermore, if Dillon fell ill, a penis would allow him to check into a hospital without having to explain why his genitals did not match the rest of his body. A penis, along with the beard and the pipe, would hide his history, keep his secret that much safer. Dillon feared, above all, the tabloids. If the rumor got out that Michael Dillon, brother to a Baronet, had once been a girl, the gossip would surely be trumpeted in every low-class newspaper in Britain. As Dillon saw it, a penis would help to safeguard his privacy and his family's honor.

So during the mid-1940s, Dillon lived a curious double life: he was both a medical student in Dublin and a patient in England. During the university term, he shadowed doctors on their hospital rounds, assisted in the surgical theater, and even performed an appendectomy. When the term ended, Dillon would ride a train through the English countryside to a small town called Basingstoke, home to Rooksdown House, the hospital overseen by Sir Harold Gillies...

Sir Harold, as the patients called him, understood that recovery had as much to do with the mind as the body. Some of the patients at Rooksdown were so disfigured that, even with the best care, they would remain outcasts for the rest of their lives....Dillon thrived at Rooksdown. He befriended a man with plastic ears, [a] girl who'd been scalped by a factory machine, and the Navy officer who'd had his genitals ripped off by the gears of a machine. Stunted by years of ridicule, Dillon flowered in the tolerant atmosphere of Rooksdown: he turned witty, expansive, even popular. Dillon regarded the hospital as a year-round summer camp for misfits, and eagerly looked forward to seeing old friends every time he returned....

In the town surrounding the hospital, local people had grown used to seeing patients without noses or jaws walking around town. At the post office or on the street, Dillon and his friends could expect smiles and hellos from the villagers. But the patients knew that once they boarded the train, they would become pariahs at the very next town—passengers would flinch, stare, scuttle away from them. Dillon had one advantage over most of the other patients: in that world beyond Basingstoke, he could pass as an ordinary man as long as he kept his clothes on. Still, this passing came at an emotional cost; a rigidly moral man, he had to lie constantly. When he returned to Dublin and ran into his fellow medical students, he had to invent stories to explain why he limped and sometimes had to walk with a cane. He blamed his troubles on the war—insinuating he'd been maimed in the Blitz, which he had not.

To keep the other students from asking questions, he cultivated a reputation as a stodgy bachelor, an older student who sequestered himself in the little house he owned. Now and then he asked young women out to dances and swooped around the floor in his white tie and tails. But Dillon didn't go on second dates. "One must not lead a girl on if one could not give her children. That was the basis of my ethics," he wrote later.[2] Ethics weren't the half of it. How many women would be willing to risk the scandal of marrying the first artificial male? None, probably. At any rate, he didn't care to risk finding out. To marry a young woman, he would have to confess too much to her: the 13 operations, the testosterone pills, the years of living as Laura. He was terrified, too, of what would happen if he ever did work up the nerve to tell a girlfriend about himself; he imagined how the smile would freeze on her face and her eyes would dart away, and how, when she looked back at him, she would no longer see him as a real man. He couldn't bear that. And so he avoided women. He brooded over the unfairness of his fate—it seemed he'd been given manhood, only to be denied a wife and children.

Still, he loved the way he looked in his tie and tails; he enjoyed a night of dancing, and an evening of playful flirting eased his loneliness a bit. So he took out a nurse or female student now and then, but he never let her closer than the arm's length of a waltz. He kept his distance by treating women in a rough brotherly fashion, developing a reputation as a bit of a woman-hater. He liked to lecture his dates about how the female brain was more suited to housework than intellectual pursuits—a strategy guaranteed to stifle any romance.

Dillon claims that his misogyny was all an act, one of the tools he used to keep women from falling in love with him. But, in fact, he did believe the female mind to be a strange and rather frightening organ. Women had hurt him, over and over, even before the sex change. In Laura Dillon's teenage and university years, she had fallen in love with at least two straight women. Both of them had pushed Laura away. The worst part was that these would-be-sweethearts had regarded her as a lesbian rather than as the man she wanted to be. ... So, women could not be trusted. Dillon had learned this early on. By age 35, he had vowed never to fall in love.

And then Roberta Cowell [a pre-op transwoman] slid into the seat across from him at [a] London restaurant, and he dared to hope again. ... He had decided, from the logic of his profound isolation, that Cowell must be his soul mate. Dillon was lonely in the way we can all recognize, and he also suffered from a brand-new, twentieth century solitude, too, one that had never existed before—the loneliness of a medical miracle, of the person who has experienced unique states of mind and body. He'd dared to confide in so few friends, and even the kindest of them had never really understood.

But now he shared a table with the first person he'd ever met who'd entered that blur of hormones, who planned to transform her body just as he had. She relied on him, he liked to believe, not just as a doctor, but also as a man...who could guide her through difficulties. Dillon, too, had endured the torment of the in-between period when the hormones began pushing his body toward androgyny; he knew what it was like to stumble through a city street where passersby stared at him.... Whenever Dillon traveled to London, he made sure to call on her.

At one of these early meetings, "He...whipped out the penis, which he was very proud of" wrote Cowell. "It wasn't any kind of seduction scene. He just wanted me to see what medical science had achieved. I had never seen anything like it. It was huge, and in a constant state of semi-erection." She made a joke about [his penis] being rough-hewn. [Dillon] did not laugh.... "Dillon did not exactly have the most perfectly developed sense of humor," according to Cowell. Though, really, how could he have laughed? He'd unzipped for her: he'd showed her the evidence of his excruciating pain, all those operations and infections. He'd wanted her to see how he'd turned that suffering into a handsome piece of flesh. And all she could do was snigger. Still, he refused to be discouraged. In his terrible loneliness, Roberta Cowell began to haunt his thoughts....

It was 1951 now; Cowell had turned herself into a va-va-voom peroxide blonde.... [Dillon] took it for granted that they would marry.... Besides, as Dillon saw it, he was the only man she *could* marry. Once she had gone through her final surgery, they would be the only postoperative transsexuals in all of Britain.... Separately, they were two people who each guarded a secret, each of whom could be destroyed by a rumor or a tenacious reporter. Together, married, they would be much safer, much less likely to be exposed by the press; they would become blessedly invisible; just another frowsy heterosexual couple. That was Michael Dillon's ambition: to be ordinary. To melt into the crowd. He wrote to tell her that as soon as he passed his examinations and became a doctor, they would go ahead and marry.... His most pressing worry was his medical exams, which he thought he might fail. He felt he should have a job as a doctor—or the promise of one—before he asked [Roberta] to marry him.... He wore his lucky Oxford tie on the day of the final examination. The tie did its work: Dillon passed. He had become, to his own astonishment, a licensed doctor....

If Dillon married and raised some adopted children, if he managed to shake off the reputation as a loner, he could do more than just pass as a born male. He would feel like one, too. Like so many other people in the 1950s, Dillon had enormous hopes for the institution of marriage. It would be the badge of his citizenship, a passport into the land of the ordinary. But would [Roberta] have him? Would she agree to recognize the penis Gillies had made—that organ that had once inspired her hoots of laughter—as a penis indeed?

Several years before, in his book *Self*, Dillon had argued that transsexuals were ordinary people who just happened to be trapped in the wrong body. With the right surgeries and pills, he insisted, these people could become model citizens. It was a blazingly original idea in a time when most of the top medical minds still had no idea that transsexuals existed.

In *Self* Dillon argued [that] the transsexual patient need[ed] "his body [to fit his mind"; this was the only therapeutic model that would work for him. Transsexuals could not be talked out of their urges; psychiatry would not help. It was their bodies that didn't fit, and so the only cure was to give the patient a new body.

Two decades later, Dr. Harry Benjamin would say much the same thing—only he would say it in much clearer language to a far broader audience. Benjamin, lifted to prominence by his famous friend Christine Jorgensen, became known as *the* expert on transsexuality in the 1950s—indeed, he is often credited with coining the term *transsexual* even though others had used the word before him. When Benjamin died at the age 101, the *New York Times* described him as the "first student of transsexualism to discern that it was different from homosexuality or transvestism—phenomena with which it was often confused." He also saw that transsexuals required medical assistance.

In fact, the credit for these insights should properly go to Michael Dillon, who stumbled toward the same revelations during the early 1940s. Though Dillon was the first, he was never recognized as such. His obscure book, *Self*, reached only a small readership. At the time Dillon wrote, no surgeon in England or the United States would admit to performing a sex-change operation. Both countries had laws (the so-called mayhem statute) that forbid anyone from mutilating a man who could be drafted as a soldier—so physicians refused to amputate healthy testicles lest they be hauled into court. Laws aside, doctors were leery of operating on bodies to fix what they viewed to be a psychological condition, a mere neurosis. They'd sworn, under the Hippocratic Oath to do no harm. Harm, back then, included sex-change operations.

Dillon argued for a new kind of medical morality, one that took into account the patient's deepest urges. He'd met men at Rooksdown who'd had their faces burned into a red mask during war. These men would never have sweethearts or jobs unless their faces could be fixed. Transsexuals confronted the same situation; they felt stuck in deformed bodies that humiliated them. He insisted that the sex-change operation was not a violation of the Hippocratic Oath—instead, it was a necessary treatment for people who needed to have their misshapen body restored to wholeness. Dillon had argued that if transsexuals were given the right body their troubles would end; he set out to prove this point with his own life. In 1950, he—and his surgeon Gillies—believed he would settle down, sober up, marry, and muddle on as an ordinary man.

Of course, it's a hard job for anyone to act ordinary for years on end. The trouble for Dillon was he couldn't seem to stop editing his identity. When the sex-change was behind him and his body sculpted to his satisfaction, Dillon decided to modify his mind. He pored over the books written by mystics in an attempt to calm his whirling thoughts and refurbish his personality. When books didn't save him, he pursued extreme treatments.... His longing pulled him to India, years before hippies began beating a path there, in search of some final transformation. "The conquest of the body proved relatively easy," he observed at the end of his life. "But the conquest of the mind is a never-ending struggle."

Dillon's tale proves just how far a human being can bend, how protean we are, how raw with possibility. He inhabited a dizzying array of roles: schoolgirl, doctor, besotted suitor, sailor, mystic. And yet, no matter how much he managed to mold his body and mind, Dillon could never manage to blot out a certain stubborn nub of himself, an essential quirk of his personality. Dillon could never change his desire for change.

Endnotes

1   This biographical sketch was taken from Pagan Kennedy's biography of Michael Dillon, *The First Man-Made Man: The Story of Two Sex Changes, One Love Affair, and a Twentieth-Century Medical Revolution*, (New York: Bloomsbury, 2007), out of print.

2   Michael Dillon, "Out of the Ordinary" (unpublished manuscript), 70.

A Guided Tour through Phalloplasty[1]

Martin Kincaid

I would like to share with readers...my personal experience of the journey through radial forearm free-flap phalloplasty. Anyone contemplating phalloplasty in any serious sense of the word would be well-advised to educate themselves completely. The individual should have reasonable expectations of [the] outcome and sound reasons for undergoing this most complex surgery. I believe one must be well-motivated and committed to a plan of action that will help ensure a successful overall outcome.

I chose to do a tremendous amount of research in various medical libraries. Having some medical background helped in deciphering the complex medical terminology...In addition, I spoke and met with individuals who were undergoing or had undergone some form of phalloplastic surgery. I also spoke and met with several surgeons around the country who specialize in phalloplasty. I stayed with a friend who had recently undergone a radial forearm free-flap phalloplastic procedure technique, and witnessed first-hand the results, his fears, pain and complications. This was an excellent opportunity to get close to the true reality of another's personal journey to fulfillment. Each individual has his own unique circumstances and responses, but experiencing another's journey is probably as close as you can get until you experience your own.

Another factor when embarking on this process is how it will be paid for and how much financial expense will be incurred. Contrary to popular opinion, many insurance companies have paid some if not all expenses associated with this procedure. Yet, even companies that have done so for one policyholder may deny another. One factor in the decision-making process is the type of policy. It is crucial that one read and understand their policy thoroughly and be willing to resubmit their claim and if possible take the insurance company to court. The old adage, "The squeaky wheel gets the grease" is certainly true in this case.

Medicare insurance to this day flatly denies any claims regarding gender alteration. However, the states' Medicaid programs have been known to pay for these services on an individual basis. There is some case history on this in the law libraries. Many times it is necessary to fight a legal battle to obtain coverage. More progressive states, such as Minnesota, are more lenient in granting sex change procedures and tend to pay higher rates to hospitals and physicians.

This brings me to another point: Medicaid in general pays very poorly, and many physicians may refuse to perform surgery at such a drastically reduced rate if you win your case under Medicaid.

I myself have been blessed beyond my wildest dreams—but not without a long, tedious, embittered battle with New Jersey Medicaid. Sheer will and determination cannot be long denied. I had the benefit of a pro bono lawyer, the testimony of my therapist, and letters from surgeons all across America to help me produce a precedent-setting case in granting the first known request for phalloplasty in the state of New Jersey under the Medicaid program. I had already selected the surgeons I deemed the best in this country who had given me wonderful letters of support that were instrumental to my court appeal...I can give only the highest praise possible to my team of physicians for granting me a new lease on life which otherwise would not have been afforded...The care I received at both hospitals was outstanding. My experience has been an adventure and challenge, and I have absolutely no regrets.

June 2, 1993, a day that remains indelibly imprinted on my mind, was the day I waited for my whole life—to realize the complete physical transformation of my being. One would probably expect to be quite nervous anticipating a surgical procedure that would take 20 hours, but there was a quiet calm within me and an assuredness that I had done everything conceivable to pave the way to surgical success. I had quit smoking, after being a smoker for 26 years, because most surgeons say that smokers run many risks with healing and circulatory problems. Some individuals have completely lost their penises through some necrosis (tissue death), for which smoking can be a deciding culprit. Nationwide, 10% of free-flap procedures end up with varying degrees of necrosis, another 2-3% are saved. I believe this success rate can be attributed to the surgeons' skills and the monitoring system that is meticulously set in place post-op. A dopler is utilized hourly to check the pulse in the neo-phallus. By monitoring the health of the penis on a frequent basis, the physicians are able to keep complications to a minimum.

When I woke up in Intensive Care I was in tremendous pain and vomiting projectilely. I had a morphine drip at my disposal, but the morphine seemed to increase my nausea and I was quite cognitive enough to work the drip effectively. Each individual has their own tolerance for pain; I assume in most cases pain can be well-controlled. I endured pain because I didn't know any better and believed that the morphine could only do so much. At the time I did not realize that what I was experiencing was out of the norm. I therefore advise voicing your complaints.

My left forearm, wrist and fingers felt as if nails were being driven through them, and there was a tingling numb sensation in the majority of my hand. The left forearm had been chosen as the donor site, which is usually utilized for a variety of reasons…The vessels in the forearm fit well to those that would be hooked up in the groin. The tissue is easier to work with… There is less hair on the inner surface, making this flap a good choice for urethral construction. Hair in the urethra is to be avoided as it can cause the formation of stones…

The creation of a urethra is probably the most challenging, complicated aspect of this surgery. The surgeon strips away the skin on the side of the little finger. From forearm to wrist this tissue is de-epithelized (its protective surface is removed); it is then folded around itself to create a tube which will become the neo-urethra. On the opposite side of the forearm behind the thumb another tube is created to house the penile implant. What appear at the end of this process are two tubes within a tube. Nerves, arteries and veins are dissected and repaired. While one team is creating the neo-phallus another team is preparing the recipient site.

If a hysterectomy has not been performed it will be now. It may even be best not to have a hysterectomy prior to this, as the physicians do have a preferred method to preserve nerves and eliminate scarring. In addition, Dr. Lawrence Gottlieb can perform a procedure to take part of the abdominal rectus to build a large scrotum. A vaginectomy is performed, removing the vagina and its glands. The labia minora are utilized to form an extension to the native urethra. This is one of the tricky parts: as a male hook up, the problems associated with this construction can easily result in strictures, which is a narrowing of the urethra (usually due to scar tissue) which could ultimately result in the inability to void. Surgical intervention may be necessary to restore urinary function if catheterization and dilation are unsuccessful. Because it takes hundreds—if not thousands—of stitches, layer upon layer, the likelihood of fistulas forming is an ever great concern. A fistula is an unnatural opening or exit to the outside of the body or another bodily organ. My fistulas occurred at this common junction of the urethral hook-up. I had four holes at the base of my penis. Sixty-percent of these fistulas require surgical intervention; fortunately, I was in the 40% who self-heal. The head of the penis is also created at the time of this initial surgery. The labial tissues are repositioned and sewn together to create a scrotum complete with mid-line raphne.

In addition to the above complications, infections, hematomas (pooling of blood), and stones are not uncommon. I had a hematoma due to a failed wall in the hook-up of my urethra. I also had urinary tract infections, and a staph infection that was caught and treated immediately. In addition to surgery to correct the hematoma, I underwent carpal tunnel surgery in the donor arm. Carpal tunnel syndrome and other neuropathics associated with donor site complications are not generally the norm. However, some individuals may have propensity for this type of complication. I've gone through months of physical therapy to restore strength and minimize the hypersensitivity in my hand. There is still presently some residual numbness and tingling.

The drawback to utilizing the non-dominant forearm for a graft is the large, and many believe unsightly, scarring. I am pleased with the healing of my forearm, and from an aesthetic perspective it doesn't bother me. Some may also consider this donor site unacceptable as the length of one's penis will be dependent on the length of their particular forearm. Most patients will end up with a penis five to seven inches in length. The fat content in the forearm has some bearing on how much girth the new penis will have. In addition, the donor site can more than likely be reconstructed through the technique of tissue expansion if one is distressed by the loss of forearm bulk and scarring.

The average stay in the hospital for this long and complicated procedure is 10 to 14 days. My stay was three weeks with an additional one week readmission for the carpal tunnel surgery and the reinsertion of a catheter that had broken. I initially awoke on June 3rd with a supra-pubic catheter (a catheter inserted directly into the bladder) which then act[ed] as a catheter to drain the urine. Also, my penis had a Foley catheter that initially provide[d] a mechanism to maintain the urethral tunnel. Later, urine [was] diverted through this Foley catheter, but initially no stresses [were] desired on the penis…

My Foley catheter was in place for approximately three months due to the delayed healing of fistulas. The process of catheterization contributes to urinary tract infections and bladder spasms. I found catheterization very uncomfortable and inconvenient. It necessitates wearing a leg bag when up and around, emptying and cleaning the bags. Still, if I had to do it all over again, I would do so without hesitation. I stayed in Chicago for over two months because of the instability of my catheterization. My supra pubic catheter, which was stitched into my abdomen, continually broke loose and had to be stitched several times. Eventually, it completely worked its way out. Fortunately by then I was able to void through the penile catheter. Through my experience and from knowing others who have gone through this surgery, you will not want to or be able to run around, lift weights, or resume your normal course of daily activities for several weeks or months post-op. Complications are the norm and patience will go a long way in the healing process.

Another complication that can occur, though rare, is anterior compartment syndrome. I have a very good friend who suffered this casualty in both legs. He has undergone many surgeries to restore function in his legs. This condition can arise because the legs do not get complete circulation and are put in a compromised position for a very extended period of time. Surgeons take precautions to avoid this problem but no one can guarantee completely successful results, and as long as people are human, mistakes will happen…

Because I had been on a catheter for so long, when it was eventually removed I became incontinent…and had to use Depends…for a few days. My fear of permanent incontinence was relieved by Dr. Gottlieb, who informed me that this surgery does not include the native urethral sphincter and so the problems [would] resolve in a short time.

During one of my follow-up visits I requested that Dr. Levine scope my urethra just to make sure everything was in order. It was discovered…that I had urinary tract polyps, a stricture, and residual stones from a long period of catheterizations. I was operated on through laser surgery to remove this problem and was released the same day.

In August 1994 I chose to have a penile pump implant inserted so I could engage in sexual intercourse. I was orgasmic through manual stimulation four months post-op and at this point I had fairly good sensation except for the dorsal (top) aspect of my penis, which had necessitated utilizing a flap of natural genital tissue that never developed sensation. This flap isn't normally used, but the fat content in my forearm had been underestimated and normal procedural closure had been impossible. I was in the hospital four to five days for this implant procedure. Immediately upon awakening I found that complete sensation on the right side of my penis had been knocked out. My surgery had been complicated due to the fact that I had a tremendous amount of scar tissue that had to be cut away. In addition, I had a particularly long nerve that tended to coil. Instinctively, I felt that this condition was not going to self-correct. Only time [would] tell, as it [could] take six months or more for a nerve to begin to regenerate. This side of my penis had been the more sensate side. Still, I did not mourn my loss and believed there would be a solution to the problem.

Dr. Levine utilizes a technique that he has developed to help prevent extrusion of the implant and erosion or tip necrosis. He creates a sleeve made from gortex which is a substance acceptable to the body…He inserts the cylinder of the implant into the sleeve which is then anchored to the pubic bone which also provides some stability…[Natal] penises will accommodate two cylinders…Because a reconstruction does not have these corporal bodies two cylinders are advised against. One patient went against these recommendations and suffered some loss of sensation. Yet, I followed typical procedure and lost half of my available sensation. There just aren't any guarantees in life. Always weigh the risks to the possible rewards when making decisions.

Most physicians do not have the expertise to perform successful penile implant procedures in a completely reconstructed penis. Some will lie and say it simply can't be done. As a matter of fact, a team of doctors who told me several years ago that it was impossible have finally hopped on the bandwagon and started to insert prostheses in the 40-odd penises they had already crafted. They decided to change the methodology of the procedure and experienced a very high failure rate.

In order to be a good candidate for this procedure, one should wait a long enough time for healing and hopefully complete sensation to occur, or at least acquire sensation at the tip of the penis (approximately one year). During this procedure a pump is inserted into one side of the scrotum, a cylinder is inserted into the shaft of the penis and a reservoir is placed under the stomach muscles. When the bulb of the pump is squeezed several times, the saline in the reservoir is transported into the cylinder in the penis, adding erection. When sexual activity is completed the opposite rectangular side of the pump is squeezed and held to release the saline back into the reservoir housed under the abdominal muscles. Again there are risks associated with this, as with any surgery.

I had been self-catheterizing with a device called an entrac catheter since about October 1993. Initially I was instructed to insert a deflated cylinder covered with K-Y jelly into my penis until I felt it enter my bladder—at the opposite end of the cylinder was a syringe filled with water. Squeezing the syringe filled the deflated cylinder and expanded the urethra. This was in place for ten minutes every day. Eventually, one is weaned off this exercise. I have not self-catheterized since my implant surgery of August 1994. Hopefully, my situation will remain stable and there will never be a need to do so again.

After receiving my implant I was instructed to perform another exercise a few weeks post-op. I would pump up the implant and keep it erect for 15 minutes twice a day. This apparently helps to encapsulate the implant in the tissue and also helps one to become adept at being ready at a moment's notice. I was also instructed to tug on the pump housed in my scrotum and milk the shaft gently in an effort to wet the implant and pump. I experienced intercourse for the first time on New Year's Eve 1994 in a romantic Atlantic City setting. Though I was unable to orgasm, the experience was nonetheless thrilling. Because of my current sensation deficits I have trouble knowing when I fall out of my lover's vagina. Also, some possibilities are difficult if not impossible because my penis seems not to have enough rigidity at its base. The use of two condoms helps firmness, yet further hinders sensation. Regardless, I will be patient and find alternatives if not solutions.

At the present writing (March 26, 1995) I am recuperating in a Chicago patient hotel room. I was operated on March 13th for seven and a half hours. The coronal ridge was formed on the head of my penis, the scarred insensate genital flap was removed, my scrotum was enlarged through a tissue flap harvested from my left inner thigh, [and] my penis was made more circular as it had a flat wedge-type shape before. The base was reduced, hopefully helping with some rigidity. And since I was opened, the nerve damage was explored, and found to be trapped in a bed of scar tissue. It took so long to locate the nerve that swelling of my penis made it impossible to perform a primary closure and another skin graft had to be harvested from my right inner thigh in order to close the surgical incisions. Still, there is no guarantee this partial nerve release will bring back sensation. However, at the present I feel some internal sensation where there has not been before. I feel confident that time or possibly another surgical procedure introducing a new nerve into the area will eventually bring more erotic sensation into my penis. This time I stayed in the hospital eight days. I had some delayed healing and because I have an implant that could possibly get infected the doctor took the proper precautionary measures. If surgical procedures go too deep and depose the implant, there is the possibility of infection that may necessitate removal of the device as it generally does not tend to self-correct. I am in God's hands and am confident I will continue to survive. My penis looks like dog meat, what with its many shaded bruises and blackened head, a skin graft that is oozing and raw, and blisters to boot—but still, it is my penis, with God's help it will heal.

. . ..

(April 23, 1995) I feel compelled to add to my original letter. I have experienced a rare and devastating setback. The blackened areas on my penis, which were believed to most likely heal on their own or with some slight debridement (scraping away of dead tissue), turned out to be much more serious. I was readmitted to the hospital for another 22-day stay, and have undergone two more surgeries. Unfortunately, I lost half of my penis and much of its larger girth. My once large member looks to me now like a pea shooter (no pun intended).

One positive result of my misfortune is that the doctors have broadened their base of knowledge. The pattern of necrosis revealed to them that any revisions should be made prior to the placement of the penile implant.

The tissue around the implant had become ischemic (lacking oxygen due to compromised blood flow) and had become necrotic…I remember posing my question to my doctors over a year ago: "Would it matter if the penile implant surgery was selected before doing aesthetic revisions?" My doctor did not believe at that time that it would make any difference. He now knows that it can indeed make a world of difference.

Needless to say, I suffered the usual feelings of denial, depression, anger and frustration that anyone would suffer with major loss. I was wise enough to seek the counsel of the hospital staff psychologist in working through these feelings and, surprisingly, I had entered into the acceptance stage within a week postoperatively. When I wrote my original letter I never believed that at this stage of the game I would have to go through those experiences I found to be less than comforting. I am again on a supra-pubic catheter and a Foley catheter. During my readmission to the hospital the doctors were initially unable to get a Foley catheter completely into my bladder. A cystogram revealed some form of the blockage (initially thought to be a stricture). I was put under via a spinal anesthesia and a cystoscopy revealed a diverticulation would make it more possible to place the Foley catheter. He said that removal would not affect the flow of urine either way. However, he stated that he must be very careful, for a mistake could leave me incontinent. I said to go ahead.

In hindsight I don't know if I would have made such a casual choice if I had not been under the influence of anesthesia. I guess I won't know for certain if this procedure was a success until I am removed from these blasted catheters. This time, on these catheters, I am not using any bags. My bladder is being trained, and when I get the urge to urinate I unclasp the Foley and the urine drains out. The supra-pubic is a backup in the event that I'm unable to void normally through my pea shooter. I really think that will be no problem, as urine is flowing through my penis and the catheter now.

Now, what to do about Stubby (my small penis). My surgeon tells me this problem is not insurmountable. He must wait and see the results of healing to determine what the best course of action would be. It may be wiser to go for a full reconstruction, which include sacrificing my right forearm. He may decide to add on to Stubby or revise what I now possess. Without [knowing] all the pros and cons it is difficult for me to even begin contemplating the choices. I am exhausted from this ordeal and wonder why this had to happen to me. It is believed that this incident had less than one percent possibility of occurring. Hopefully, my misfortune will save some of your readers from this fate. Now that you have this piece of knowledge you can make more educated decisions. Still, with all my hardships and complications I do not regret that I lost what I had. However, maybe in the end I will have a result that will be better than what I would have had if these events had not taken place. In less than two years, I have undergone eight surgeries and been treated for many infections. My goal is not to discourage you from choosing phalloplasty but to show you how to reduce risks, realize the possible price, and make educated, informed decisions. I still believe that I have chosen the best team of surgeons in this country. This surgery holds the possibility of many complications. One must have the stamina, courage, hope, and fortitude to press on to one's dreams. For me it is the quality, not the quantity, of life that is most important. Even with my small ill-formed penis I am far better off than I was prior to my genital surgery. For me, anyway, the prices I have paid are still worth what I have gained.

It may be necessary to remove the implant in my scrotum (the pump). I have been experiencing quite a bit of pain since the penile cylinder had to be removed. The implant surgery bill was about $25,000. I had sex six times—that's at about $4000 a pop. Luckily, I did not pay much financially—my cost was about $500. However, I now face the possibility of not having medical insurance when and if I choose to have an implant reinstalled. Well, that decision is probably at least a year or more into the future. I must take one day at a time, for to view the total process could overwhelm me at this point.

...[M]ay your venture to and through phalloplasty be more successful than that undergone by those who have come before you. My case, fortunately, is not the norm. I have had more work and complications of my penis than any other 18-20 penises my doctors have created.

I trusted that the information I have provided has not scared you away from your dreams but has given you food for thought so you can make the choices best suited for your individual needs.

A few more words of advice I would like to offer to anyone who decides to opt for phalloplasty:

1. Have a supportive, nurturing person or persons available to help you post-operatively with personal care and wound care, someone who will understand that you may suffer from depression and irritability. The

nicest people in the world can become ornery in view of the pain, uncertainty and drugs. Also have a therapist available to help with all this.

2. Visit with as many board-wide physicians as possible who have performed this procedure successfully on a number of people. Ask to see pictures, possibly journals they've contributed to, patient referrals of people that would be willing to share their experiences. Don't enter into anything without having all your questions and concerns addressed. I personally highly recommend the doctors who performed my surgery. I have heard horror stories from several patients of other physicians, and I know for a fact that some doctors can be less than honest. Also, some doctors perform procedures strictly out of their own ego needs, not what's in your best interest.

3. Do not allow price to determine your choice of procedure or physician if at all possible. Negotiate price with the doctor you deem most appropriate for you.

4. Choose the procedure that best matches your needs and comfort level, including the choice not to undergo surgery at all.

5. Do not enter into this surgery to please a lover or anyone else. Do it because you are driven to make this change and are willing to pay the price for the possibly tremendously satisfying results.

6. Envision your arm as if it is already scarred. Envision your new penis, fully functional. If you can adjust to the scar in your mind's eye before you see it in reality your adaptation will be much easier.

7. Gather as many facts as possible but do not become paralyzed by analysis.

8. Quit smoking. Eat a balanced fortified diet with mega vitamins. Don't do drugs or alcohol, and get into your best physical shape. Lose weight if possible, if you are overweight. Get rest and relaxation. Don't let worrying of nervousness consume your energy or alter your judgment.

9. Trust in your doctors, have a good rapport with them, ask questions and inform them of anything you feel is unnatural in your healing process. Ask for pain medication or other items of comfort such as an egg crate mattress (it does wonders for your back).

10. Follow your doctors' instructions of post-op care to a "T". This is not a time for you to determine the rules of post-op care. I have witnessed the complications that can result when one alters accepted protocol.

11.   Pray and have others pray for your successful and speedy recovery. Be patient, have faith and endure the hardships, for the winter will eventually turn into spring.

12.   If insurance coverage is unavailable, negotiate fees with your doctors and the hospitals. Ask to be put on a lifetime payment plan if necessary.

13.   If a staff member neglects to perform a service such as emptying your urine bag or rehooking the leg compression devices, gently remind them that this is your body and someone else's errors can affect your life.

14.   Plan to stay in the area at least some of the time after release from the hospital—you will need to see your doctors post-op, and it is comforting to know they're only a cab ride rather than a plane ride away.

15.   Do not believe those who declare that a functional penis is impossible to construct. My research, though a small sampling, indicates that those individuals who had the psychological need for a sensate penis that was also capable of urination and intercourse were more satisfied with the results than those who choose the old Stanford abdominal flap method. It is technically possible today to have it all—even though there are few doctors able to skillfully provide it.

16.   Finally, don't beat your meat against the toilet seat until your doctor tells you [that] you can now enjoy that treat.

Endnotes

1   The following testimony was originally published in the July 1995 issue of *FTM International Newsletter*, which was founded by Lou Sullivan and maintained subsequently by Jamison Green after Sullivan's death.

Part II

WITNESSING
TRANSFORMATION

Gender and sex transitions bring significant life altering changes for trans people in every dimension of our lives, including our relationships with loved ones, spouses, children, parents, friends, and co-workers. The lives of others are affected in many ways, as people shift, adjust and accommodate to our changing bodies, minds, and lived realities. Yet, rarely do they have opportunities to speak and write publically about the impact of gender transitions on them and the transformations that they undergo as well. This section offers the perspectives of five significant others who write of their experience of loving trans men who surgically modified their genitals.

A Femme's Chrysalis

Isabella Abrahams

The Beginning Spark

We live in a binary plane and there is a certain acceptance of either/ or, good/evil, yin/yang. We need better options, and we are just beginning to have glimpses of the many possibilities of how gender morphs and manifests itself. We all come to this life with an agreement to experience this adventure, this three-dimensional school, starting in our own personal ocean, programmed to grow into this human body. The mother bathes us all in estrogen and progesterone in the womb causing some to go back and forth in gender assignment several times. It can be an archetypal battle, the first initiation into the hero's journey. Some lose this first battle, only to have to recreate themselves again later by taking hold of the gender reins. They ride into a new country, crossing the borders, taking a new identity, like a spy in possible enemy territory. It is not a choice, and it is brave and sometimes dangerous. To challenge convention is a revolutionary stance and can result in the firing squad. I hold myself as a witness and an ally and sometimes as a fellow spy. I carry the story of my beloved, like coins sewn into my clothes. And sometimes some of that story passes through my femme lips, secrets kissing the air. This is one of those moments for those ears that are ready.

The Dangerous Dance

I have always felt the most comfortable walking on the edges of cliffs, on the tops of high fences in the murky between-world, neither here nor there, but somewhere in the middle. So I looked for a partner who knows that dance and enjoys throwing me up to the clouds, secure that I may or may not come down into their arms, and that either way, it was okay. I did not really believe that I could be matched in this way until I set my eyes on my beloved, Trystan. On meeting him, I felt the call of the moment. I tried to circle slowly, but centripetal force pulled me in, a storm that I could not fight. Nor did I want to. Within minutes of meeting, we were in each other's arms, electricity lighting up the air between us. We had a forever quality about our embrace, and I had a hard time staying on the ground, which began to fall away beneath me, leaving me to walk on the edge of myself. I fell into Trystan, and we have never completely pulled our cells apart. He is my tether, allowing me to fling myself just a little over the edge, flirting with the fall.

There were ripple effects from this energetic crash into each other. Some would try to rip us apart, seeing that we are a formidable force and, we had to do spiritual battle, but the inevitability of us, built a shelter, fending off the daggers of curse. There seemed to be these rites of initiation that we had to pass to earn the right to be together. Going through this experience gave us a warp and weave of strength that has seen us through many challenges. We arrived in to each other whole individual beings, proud scars of lessons learned and earned, painted on our skin like tribal tattoos. As a femme, I have the choice to cover my scars with painted colors, a proud peacock. However, I had to watch my gender outlaw Papi layer those scars with invisible ones, those that do not show. Judgmental eyes bore invisible holes into his black butch body, as he dared to go through those prohibited gendered doors and dared to walk down a street dressed for himself and defiance of the gender police.

Being the well-trained femme, I had learned how to transform my lover's body, avoid the prohibited spaces, and carve a breast metaphorically into a chest. It was second nature to me, and I was comfortable with recreating his male identity in our butch-femme reality. This enabled me to see his surgical changes as just another episode of our imagined gender dimorphism.

Gemini that he is, moreover, I had become quite comfortable with relating to several diverse personas all wrapped in one body. It was/is like being in a relationship with several different people, which made it easier to process his transition as adding another persona to the already existing constellation. It had always existed as a metaphor and option in my mind, so when Trystan's physical pain began pointing us toward top surgery it was really not about transing his body. After his chest surgery, we were soon to discover a remarkable truth as the scroll rolled itself out like a red carpet welcoming us to a new premier. The truth did not have to be spoken. It floated around the room, around our home, and on the plane to Europe with us. The words came out of my mouth with a mind of their own, the color of dark molasses, taking years of moments to pass through my lips, rich and sweet. There was something between us. At first, no definition presented itself and the words just lingered, naked and raw, filling the air between us. But words can be like lovers and I found myself in a *ménage à trois*. So "something" travelled with us from country to country, as my lover left layers of skin, pain and definition behind. He came back to America, naked, new fresh skin and in transition.

I wear metaphoric glasses that allow me to sanctify the mundane. Everything that we do in the same place at different moments of time, over and over again become ritual. So many aspects of transition are ritual and I proclaim myself as witness of this process, anchoring transmutation into the blood and bones.

Dreaming and Speaking in the Shift

Change does not happen until it is imagined, called in, made manifest. So many words and dreams were shared between our lips, laid down in a bed of contemplation. The dance of negotiation is a sexy sharp edged tango, and stiletto heels wound. I believed that I could not move into acceptance beyond top surgery. But I learned what I can stretch into, as challenge knocks on my door, and over time I shifted into a new agreement with myself and Trystan. I have always prided myself on the ability to transfigure reality, and I took this as another magical challenge. To do this, I had to ask my soul some important questions. My soul reminded me that we are energetic beings choosing physical bodies to experience lessons. So, I moved out of these worldly definitions, up and out of my femme dyke persona and I saw this being that

I loved so dearly through new eyes. Gender was simply the wrapping of this beautiful package of soul seed. From this perspective I could see that I chose this journey to learn about this level of love and a new gratitude sat gently on my fear of this change. Without this calling, I may not have had the opportunity to shed my own layers and boxes. I cannot always hold this, and like everything in life it is a work in progress. I have times when I long for the comforts of my past perceptions. But in a world where we are learning to surf the tsunamis, change must become a dear friend in order to avoid becoming a fearsome foe. It is a fractal of a shift and reflection of something so much larger and timeless.

Quetzalcoatl

The operating table is a sacrificial altar: the anesthesia, an inauthentic swap for shamanic journey, the surgical tools, a bloodletting that culminates in the sacrifice of one life for another. This is the initiation that I have seen my Papi through so many times now.

For thousands of years, bodies have been laid upon altars ready for dying into a new resurrected self and sacrificed to the necessity of change. I count my beloved among these souls, laid on foreign tables in far-away lands. It is difficult to put into words the terror of watching him go into the long twilight of surgery, passing him into the great architect of no time, where anesthesia takes one. I call my Papi the rain god, as he is so enamored of the sexy wetness of storm and the spark of lightning. So it is apropos that a storm raged on through the many hours of his surgical journey, so loud that it drowned out everything except for my tears. Rain and I wailed like mothers over graves. So many hours passed—six, seven, eight—that it seemed impossible that that he could emerge unscathed. Nothing could have prepared me for my first sight of him coming out of the operating room. It seemed like there was no life present in him, color having left his mocha skin and leaving him looking like a corpse. I laid my hands on him giving every spark of life I could pull from Source, and I watched him return to me slowly. His first words were "gratitude," which he repeated over and over for several minutes, reaching out to the surgeon and myself. So, on that day, the great serpent was made manifest, harkening great changes to come. I have been a snake charmer before, and will be again. I am not going to pretend that there have not been adjustments to this new life, and it is not always easy to hold a snake. But remember that the snake holds the sacred secrets and hisses them in its own time.

Transmogrifrication

Animal joined us now though, with the new strength and rawness of testosterone coursing through his body. His need to chew and gnaw and growl brought an ineffable pre-verbal level to our erotic communication. It also brought me to my own levels of transition which was unexpected. Something grew within the lacy leather of my femme self, not about gender, but about lioness self-definition. There was never a question that I would remain a femme dyke. The outlands that I live in allow for this, as many in my tribe reside in these unexplainable complexities. Testing this beyond these safe radical limits of the Bay Area is uncharted territory, excepting travels where I use glamour hypnosis to banish the mendacity of blending in like a camouflaged lizard, spitting just a little too much glitter in others' eyes. Well, this is the story I tell myself, creating the only fabulous world I can live in. So I search for that spark of visual recognition from my sisters doing the transition tango with their lovers. We are a secret society with our own rituals and initiation is not for the faint hearted. Conformity attempts penetration, returned to its sender like a laser meant to redefine the molecules of matter. We are here to re-write the world, the possibility of transmutation glowing in the reflection of new windows to new worlds.

A New Street Dance

The Sephardim Jewish skin that I live in is a form fitting sexy dress of privilege. When I choose, I can invoke the cloak of invisibility that allows me to dance around judgments and assumptions. I am allowed to look others in the eye with my magic looking glass without invoking fear, and I have the magical keys to the forbidden gates of knowledge cities that take pride in exclusivity. I am fortunate and humble with these offered gifts, and I try not to take them for granted, and to use them for benefit of all. I have come to see that a responsibility comes with this in my relationship. My lover has turned himself inside out to reveal the black man that tried to form in the womb.

This brave decision has thrown him into a world of being feared and judged, way before he walks close enough to be known for his true self. Part of my spiritual contract with my love is finding ways to protect him, without emasculating him. At my best, I can try to hold up my superpower gauntlets and wave off the sharp knives of racist innuendo, the bitter tongues of hate. I can act as ambassador for the country of our relationship when soldiers advance. I can distract with crystal houses built with femme glitter that transport us to safer lands.

And so I commit myself to this contract, with my body and my soul. The bridges that we build today take us into our evolutionary future. The brave and amazing metamorphosis that surrounds me is only the beginning of what we are all destined to become. All parts moving into wholeness.

Fringe Benefits

Dr. Laura

I don't really remember discussing bottom surgery with my husband. When he began his journey of physical transition, I chose to support whatever he decided to do with it. It wasn't my place to give an opinion unless asked and I didn't get a vote in it. He always includes me, but I felt because it was his body, it was his decision. My role was to support and love him regardless. I have never had any fears about what his transition meant for us. He needs to be the man he knows he is and because I love him, I accept him completely.

Surgery didn't really matter that much to me. We had a great sex life before any of his surgeries, and I never really cared one way or the other. After every surgery though, our emotional connection strengthened, the sex got better, and I realized how truly important it is to him to be the man he knows himself as. I benefit from his feeling more complete because he is able now to connect with me even better than before.

My hardest time in the surgery process was that he was going to Serbia for surgery, and I couldn't be there with him. Our daughter was only one year-old at the time and it didn't make sense to leave her without access to either of us. And although he never came right out and said this, I don't think he wanted really me to be there. Of course, he wouldn't have refused if I had insisted, but I knew that it was something that he needed to do on his own, with his best (male) friend, and come back to us afterwards. It felt like a sacred rite of passage. Throughout his transitional process I never wanted to get in the way, because so many people hold back from transitioning because of what others will think about them and how they will treat them. I love him too much for that.

When my husband returned home from surgery I worried about hurting him. He was in intense pain and the thought of even accidentally brushing up against him was terrifying. When he had top surgery, I was obsessed with a fear of his nipples falling off and similar feelings resurfaced once he returned from Serbia. What if I did something inadvertently to hurt him?

He finally let me examine him following surgery once the catheters were removed. I was looking over his penis and balls and pulled on what I thought was a hair at the end of his penis. It wasn't a hair but a stitch that hadn't yet dissolved. He screamed. I screamed. I nearly passed out on the spot and he looked like he might too. I felt badly about the pain I caused him. We can laugh about it now, but we still cringe when we remember that moment.

We moved into sex slowly after surgery. It's been almost three years since his surgery, and I am still trying to figure out how hard or firm I can touch him or suck on him. He has been patient with me during my process. I think he would prefer that I be more assertive with him, harder, or firmer, but I hold back. I'm learning to get beyond my fears.

My husband did not tell his family about his surgery, but my side of the family has always known and supported us. I would characterize our family's outlook like this: when extended family of mine have asked personal questions about his physical transition, my mother fields questions with this response: "You know, we don't talk about anybody else's penis in the family, so I really don't think we need to talk about his!" And they have all stopped and respected that boundary. I am infinitely grateful to my mom for her perspective.

Initially, I did not think that it would matter whether he had surgery or not, but it has mattered a great deal. Not because I had any problems with how he was (physically) before, but because he is so much more of himself now, and we connect more deeply. My own sense of my sexuality has grown because of that connection. He has always had a male energy to me, but that male energy has gotten stronger and it's hard to resist. I identify as bi and so I like both feminine and masculine aspects of people, but he is all male, and I love that.

I have realized during his physical transition that monogamy has become less and less important for a few reasons. I have never believed that relationships hinge on monogamy. But in particular for him, I do not want to hold him back from experimenting sexually and being with other women in the body he now has. He did not get that time of experimenting like most bio guys do, and I think it is important. I love his body and what he can do with it, and I do not want to imagine him getting old and regretting not being able to know what it feels like to be with other women. I know him well enough that he would never do anything to hurt me or our family, so whatever he does with anyone else, sexually or otherwise, isn't a threat to me.

I don't know if I can offer any advice for other partners, but if I had something to add, it would be this: don't let your own stuff get in the way of your partner's quest for his own identity. It can scare you, but if you let your fears stop his process both of you will lose in the end. I need my partner to feel whole and happy and bring his whole self to our relationship. Thankfully, surgery has made that possible.

Gifts and Talents

Deborah Weekley

My spouse is Reverend David Weekley and he is a transsexual man. He transitioned over 36 years ago and has had all of his surgeries, including phalloplasty. I met David while serving on a Gang Task Force Committee in 1994 at my local Chamber of Commerce. We had similar values, and we were the only two members of the committee who wanted to help the gang members, rather than just move them out of town. Over the months we served together on this committee a friendship began to grow. We discussed many topics, including human sexuality. I had become a Christian at the age of 17 and had been evangelized by a non-denominational group in Portland, Oregon. At that time, I had no understanding of the many ways that scripture could be interpreted. What I heard and embraced was the concept of a God that loved and created all humankind and sent a guy (God's son) named Jesus to teach us to love ourselves and one another. I was involved in this church group for many years, but I began feeling uncomfortable because I disagreed with some of their hypocritical theological views of women and LGBT people. I am a heterosexual female and have always been an ally of LGBT people and causes and have many LGBT friends as well.

By the time I met David, I had been out of organized religion for many years. I had never stopped believing in God but I preferred to maintain a private relationship with my Creator instead. I had had a recent spiritual epiphany during prayer of hearing in my spirit, "Go and find a church and give of your gifts and talents." I give this background information because it is an important part of our story. I believe with my entire being that God exists and cares about justice for all people including LGBTQ people, and that much of the bigotry and discrimination against them comes from persons who have embraced a form of religion based on misinterpretations of scripture. David and I have been called to share our story publically for a reason: to be a bridge and let the world know that a transsexual man can be a Christian, a wonderful pastor, husband, father, community member and human being.

About seven months into our friendship, David revealed to me in a conversation about Christianity and LGBTQ issues that "he had been born all screwed up." I asked him what that meant and he explained about having been born anatomically as a girl, but that he had always seen himself as male. He had transitioned many years earlier with hormones and surgeries. I could tell this was a big deal that he was sharing this truth with me, as he was shaking during our conversation. But I was not negatively affected by his revelation. In fact, I felt great compassion in that moment and honored by his trust.

I had heard the term "hermaphrodite" and asked him some questions to determine if this was what he was describing. That conversation led to many more on the subject as our friendship grew. Penile construction surgery (phalloplasty) was not a new concept for me. I knew a relative who had been in a motorcycle accident a few years earlier and had severely damaged his penis. He had to undergo corrective surgery and had a permanent erection, which he was often teased about by his siblings. Over the next few years David's marriage ended, and our friendship continued to grow into a deep love and respect for one another. Eventually, we became engaged and got married on May 18, 1996.

The first time David and I made love, his body and penis surprised me. David had scar tissue on his abdomen and right upper thigh from skin grafts taken to form his penis. These scars do not bother me; rather they cause me to appreciate how much he endured to be his authentic self. Having a penis is important to him. He is in all ways male with a scrotum, testicular implants, and a lovely sized penis that *is* orgasmic and pleases me.

I had expected something more along the lines of my former brother in law: a constantly erect penis, but David's surgery was a different kind. His penis is constructed with a place to insert a prosthetic rod in the center to make it erect. This has never been a problem for me. I am grateful he has a penis and that we can be joined physically in this way during our lovemaking. I think it is more of an issue for him.

Occasionally, I have experienced him getting depressed about not having a penis that he considers normal with erectile tissue and semen. Because of this, he sometimes struggles with self-esteem and confidence issues of whether "he is enough for me." For me his depression is the greater issue. Where I am grateful he has a penis, he gets frustrated sometimes that he does not get hard like "other men" and occasionally sinks into doldrums about it. I reassure him. I remind him of the many benefits to his penis. We do not have to wait for him to get an erection. We can have intercourse for as long as we have strength. And I like not having to get up immediately and wash away semen.

Our deep love is rooted in respect and shared values. Our love making is the most beautiful and fulfilling thing I have ever experienced in my 62 years of life. We have a lot of fun making love. We experiment with positions, toys and ways of making love. One of our greatest moments came when he lost his prosthesis and it took a while to have another one made. We discovered that we did not need it. He worked just fine without a prosthetic and now we rarely use it. I realize that our experience contradicts a segment of academics in gender studies that downplays the importance of genitalia for gender identity, but David's surgery, in addition to enhancing his own sense of completeness, has allowed us to nurture and deepen our romantic, spiritual, and sexual connection. I would miss his penis if he had not had phalloplasty. However, we have been together long enough that if something happened to it, we would find other ways to pleasure one another because I love him for who he is and not because he has a functioning penis.

My advice to partners is to love and respect the person you are with and be clear about your own needs and sexual orientation. Can you celebrate your partner or spouse's gender identity? If not, be honest about it. Do not try to change someone for your own selfish needs.

My advice to transsexual men is if you were born with a female anatomy, but you are convinced you are male, do whatever you need to feel whole. It was not until David wrote and published his book, *In from the Wilderness, Sherman (She-r-man)*, that I truly understood how much he was willing to go through to be the man he is. He really does not like hospitals or hypodermic needles. His perseverance to be his authentic self was amazing to me. I cannot imagine living with the same kind of internal dissonance, but I have met many other transsexuals who do and I am convinced surgery is the only way for some people to be at peace with themselves and the world. I would advise any persons considering phalloplasty to read David's book. He is a pioneer, as his surgery was one of the first of this type in the United States. He has never doubted that it was the right path for him, and neither did the medical team that worked with him.

I celebrate my wonderful husband and am eternally grateful he had the strength of character and courage to pursue his personal truth. I am grateful that he has told his story publically. He could have continued to live in stealth, but I think his story is important in helping to change people's hearts and minds about gender identity, transitioning, and human development.

Out of the Shadows

Paula James

When my husband first told me that he was going to have surgery, I was so thrilled for both of us. I was excited for him, knowing that finally his physical, sexual equipment would reflect how he had always felt on the inside. I knew how deeply important this surgery had been for him for so many years. I have always told him that I love him for who he is, not for what was (or was not) between his legs. That still remains true today. If he had never found the time or money to go through with this change, I would still love him and be by his side forever.

I was also afraid of potential complications and all the pain and suffering that he would have to go through. He was my soul mate who was going all the way to Serbia for surgery. My first thought was, *Oh, my god, he's going into a war-torn country*. But they had stopped fighting more than a decade ago. Then I wondered: what if something went wrong and I couldn't be there to see or look after him? What happens if he dies on the table? I knew there were always possibilities of complications, and he experienced quite a few after coming home. I admit that I was a tad dramatic for my own good. But I was unable to go with him. Finances and running our business made traveling with him impossible. I knew communication was going to be spotty at best. So, quite naturally I worried about a lot of things. Occasionally, it also occurred to me that he might want to explore new sexual avenues opened up by the surgery and become curious about being with other women. How would I deal with that if it ever came up?

On another personal level, I also felt tremendous relief. At times, it has been hard emotionally to deal with my family and some of our friends who could not understand that my husband is a man, despite his birth sex and anatomy. I had been adopted and raised by a devout Mormon family who frowned on any kind of sexuality that wasn't heterosexual and procreative. My partner and I first met when we were young, 14 and 12, and much in love. But because of the Mormon Church and my family's teachings, I struggled with the issue internally and felt conflicted for many years. I did not consider myself a lesbian. Nor had I ever been attracted to women. For me, he was never a woman. He was just who he was and my heart told me that he was my soul mate. Because I was so young and naïve, I struggled to understand what loving him meant for me and who I was. I felt that his surgery would finally show the world who I really was too: that I was in love with a man and not a woman, as everyone tried to argue.

When he changed his name officially, I proudly told my adoptive parents of his plans for surgery. Yet, they continued to call him by his birth name. They refused to accept him as my soul mate and continued trying to talk me out of being with him. They wanted me to marry some "nice" Mormon boy, which was the ultimate oxymoron to me. Nice Mormon boys had sexually exploited and physically abused me, whereas my partner had only been kind and loving to me. I was crushed by my adoptive family's refusal to see that he was obviously not a lesbian. They continued to call me a lesbian for many years, and finally I told them that I no longer considered them a part of my family.

We both began to see how intolerant the public was/is about gender reassignment, and I began feeling like I had to hide from people. I was willing to do whatever it took to be with him, however, so I learned how to cope with not having friends and how to form friendships based on secrets and half-truths. It has been lonely at times, but I have also seen and dealt with the harsh consequences of disclosing anything about that part of our lives. After all, people do not need to know everything. He was concerned about my not having close friends, but just his concern at my well-being was enough to get me through lonely times. We have always been close emotionally and shared our feelings, and I knew that he too was lonely without friends. We always had each other. After a time, having close friends became less and less important for me. All I really needed was my partner and son. No matter what happened, he was supportive of me and took in my son as if he were his own and helped raise him. Without him, my son would have grown up to be irresponsible and selfish.

My husband's family was supportive. They knew who he was from the beginning and were not shocked by his decision to have surgery. In fact, they seemed to breathe a big sigh of relief for him, and if I recall, their reaction was something like "It's about time." They accepted my son and me into the family. They never made us feel like freaks as my own family had.

Initially, I was worried about being able to care for him adequately when he came back home. I was good at supporting him emotionally and helping him through his recovery. Many times I listened to him talk about his own emotional changes and what he was going through during the surgeries. I also did the usual things like changing his dressings, making sure he was eating properly, and trying to help relieve his aches and pains as best as I could. His self-confidence has increased and that is the best I could have hoped for. His confidence continued to increase in the time since the surgery. He is finally feeling more at home in his own skin. Having never gone through his experience, I will never fully understand the feelings of incompleteness that he has always felt for his entire life. But I do see the change in him emotionally, which is all the proof I need to know that he had to go through this experience to feel complete.

I love his body even more now than before, but I think that is a mental thing for me. Having never considered myself to be a lesbian or been attracted to women, I feel that I can shed any inhibitions that I may have had being with him before. He has always satisfied me, but I knew something was missing for him. I love his new penis!

My advice to other partners is to guard against taking this change as a personal affront to you as a person or a partner. His needs are not about you failing to make your partner happy. They are about your partner's body and sense of self. You are not doing anything wrong and do not need to "improve" yourself to make him happier. The best thing you can do is continue to love your partner and accept that he is doing this to feel more complete. My husband's process has never been about me. It has always been (as it should) about him finding comfort in himself. I would have been happy to spend the rest of our lives together with him, with or without surgery, but I know now that he would never have been truly happy with himself. I feel like we are walking in the sun. Before, we lived our lives hiding in the shadows, afraid to even hold hands in public for fear of the discrimination that we would get from others. I mean, if my own adoptive family who was supposed to love me unconditionally created such turmoil about this, who knows what we would have suffered from strangers. It is a joy to finally be able to hold his hand in public and not feel like we have to stick to the shadows to even look at each other as lovers. We can finally enjoy the sunshine on our faces without having to deal with people's disapproving looks.

I am so blessed to have been included in his life-changing process, and count myself lucky to go down this road with him. I would gladly go down this road with him again, regardless of all the discrimination and alienation from friends and family. It has been well worth it.

Going the Distance

Andree Culpepper

By the time we had moved our conversation from whether we would be intimate to discussing the when, he had already been through his first phase of surgery. The attraction between him and me had been smoldering for several years, but I was finally in a place emotionally where I was ready to discover what would happen if I finally let go and allowed the energy between us to be unleashed.

We first met at a workshop, and I could not resist smiling at this handsome black man who confidently returned my glances. I took as many opportunities as I could to talk to him—or perhaps harass him. We spent much of that first afternoon together in flirtatious conversation. His black skin was much darker than my own and his dread locks were lion-like; considerably longer than mine. I found his expressive eyes and big, beaming smile irresistible. As a woman of color living in the Northwest where diversity is limited, it was exciting to get an opportunity to share that lusty, sexually charged exchange with someone that shares racial commonality; almost as if we're bonded with a secret.

As the day grew closer to evening and the workshop was winding down, he clearly stepped in and took control of our conversation and its direction. The gloves were off and the sexuality became more blatant. I stumbled. My composure was lost and I languished between arousal and intimidation. Metaphorically, I had been backed into a corner, and I felt bewildered and tongue-tied. While I knew that I wanted our flirtation to continue into the night, I wouldn't give myself permission to be seduced by a man that I might never see again as he lived thousands of miles away. I didn't want to be made the fool for "giving in." I have always found pride in being one who left little room for "easy" to be included as part of my reputation. That night my stifling fear pulled me away from this man and the opportunity to let my desires get the best of me. But I can readily admit now that there were so many nights that followed in which I found myself wondering and fantasizing about what I had denied myself in order to preserve my pride.

Fortunately, his distance from me did not necessarily mean he was ever going "away." We stayed in touch by phone and saw each other once a year at an annual conference. Our talks had morphed into the kinds of discussions made between friends, but the intensity always flared during those rare occasions when we would see one another. Still, those annual visits didn't offer the opportunity that I had hoped for where I could let my guard down and allow him and myself to enjoy more than the sexual innuendo. In fact, my hesitation from our first meeting was fairly justified in my mind when he disclosed that he was married.

As I am notoriously stubborn, it mattered little how he defended his position. I knew that I was right, and I was not going to be fooled into the belief that he and his wife had "an understanding." So, naturally it took years before I could trust. Years of observing and listening to this man whom, in every situation, chose to be sincere, thoughtful, and wise. It became clear to me that his family was extremely important to him and he would do nothing to jeopardize or harm them. He showed this same love and care for me also, even while I was in relationships with other people. He would back off if I needed. I played out the idea of being with him many times in my mind, "respectful and discreet."

It was during one of our long distance conversations that we were finalizing our plans for our first opportunity to be together as sexual partners and he began to tell me about his physical body. During his slow, cautious explanation, I realized that I had assumed that his surgeries were complete. Immediately I became disappointed with myself for not having thought to approach this topic before, then somehow disappointed that it required explanation at all. I had dated a transman before, but he had made different choices for his body. The sense of feeling complete did not include bottom surgery for him and I respected that choice. However, in the present situation, I had allowed myself to fill in the blanks in my own mind. I had allowed the fantasy to carry me to this point. Now some verbal back-pedaling was in order.

They say the devil is in the details, right? I had already expressed some concerns about maybe not being able to follow through with our physical union. My initial hesitation centered on the fact that he was partnered. This was going to be my first attempt at being in an "open" relationship. I became self-conscious. What if I don't know how to touch him? What if his smell has changed and I don't like it? What if I don't get aroused? Fuck! This whole thing could have hurled us into a big awkward mess. What would I say then? I listened on the phone somewhat terrified. I don't believe I said a word to him about all my fears as he carefully continued providing details and reassured me. He offered to let me see photos. Hell no! Not a chance! I wanted to maintain any remnant of the fantasy and the mystery that I could. I got quieter on my end of the conversation. My heart was pounding hard in my chest. I was relieved that he wasn't there to see the apprehension on my face when we ended the conversation. Our rendezvous was scheduled just a few weeks away.

I had worked myself up about these concerns and I was shaking by the time I got off the plane to meet him. I stopped in the bathroom to check my face, brush my teeth, check my lipstick and fix my hair repeatedly, anything to calm my nerves and stall seeing him too soon. I kept reminding myself that I didn't have to go through with having sex with him if I didn't want to. He had been understanding about this option and even offered to let me have my own room and not even discuss the issue of sex at all the first day if I wasn't ready. While I had provided myself an "out" and relieved myself of some of my expectations at that point, I still wanted to look good for him.

I don't recall having much support during that time. I read Tristan Taormino's book, *Opening Up: A Guide to Creating and Sustaining Open Relationships*, and was trying on a new label for myself: bisexual. One afternoon I received a call from a friend whom I hadn't heard from in a long time. In order to give justice to her inquiry "What's going on with you?" I pulled over to the side of the road and matter-of-factly unloaded my feelings for ten minutes into her ear. She had moved to San Francisco the year before and, like many of my friends, had mostly been in lesbian relationships. Now, the distance gave me some safety. I couldn't physically see her reaction and judgment, but I could tell that she didn't know where to put most of what I had shared. My friends had known me to partner primarily with women so they had more questions than answers as I tried to navigate brief conversations about wanting to date a transman who was already partnered. I did attend several polyamorous discussion groups and lectures about open relationships. Listening to others in these groups, I came to understand that "open" did not mean easy.

Our airport greeting was harried and brief: a quick kiss and he took my bags. I found his scent to be nice and not overpowering. I stepped into the passenger seat of the rental car and took a few moments to remind myself to breathe. He slammed down the trunk and slid into the driver's seat. Finally he was right there next to me. I kept looking at his handsome, dark profile, then his muscular thighs. As he drove, he made almost no eye contact with me at all. After several moments, I had to touch his neck and the back of his head. He is handsome, masculine, and noticeably strong. He didn't have to say much before it became clear to me that I was going to respond well to his touch. I knew I wanted to give myself to this man.

Maybe I had worked out all the awkward possibilities by this time because, although I was still nervous, our first time was truly everything that I had wanted and needed it to be, including intense. In his own process of determining who he is, he has clearly become comfortable in his body. And, after all the years that I had stubbornly denied him the opportunity, he was ready to enjoy mine. I am a strong woman and, though fit, I am not a petite woman. He was clearly the dominant male I needed, and I felt as if I finally had permission to soften, trust, and let him take complete control. He started so gently; talking me through his actions and requests. He tried. Clearly he had planned to be careful with me, but he became less cautious, then rougher and more animal, I became more aroused and more willing to be taken. I have never felt so connected to someone else while simultaneously feeling so connected to myself as I did in those moments. Giving in to this man's desire was also giving in to my own and these were empowering moments for me. I honestly feel as if my womanhood, my femininity, is magnified when I am with him. I feel more Woman when that Man is next to me.

The perfect moment came this year when his wife, who loves him dearly, did re-define her needs and no longer wanted any outside relationships to be discreet. This gave him the opportunity to push past his own fears and share his feelings about me. It was such a relief no longer being his "secret." When we are together, we can hold hands publicly and, as the people in our lives do their best to reckon with their own realities and opinions about our situation, we have allowed ourselves to continue to transition further together and move in the direction of our personal truths.

Glossary

Abdominal panniculus—medical a fatty tissue growth, consisting of subcutaneous fat in the lower abdominal area. Abdominal panniculus can be removed during abdominal panniculectomy, a type of abdominoplasty.

Bottom Surgery—surgical alteration or (re)construction of any part of genitalia, external or internal. Also called genitoplasty, "lower surgery", "genital (re)construction" "sex reassignment surgery" (SRS), and "sex/gender affirmation (or confirmation) surgery."

Cis-gender (Cis-sexual)—"Cis" is a Latin prefix meaning: "on the same side as" or "on this side of." The terms refer to people who, unlike trans people, have always felt aligned in their gender identification, assigned birth gender, and bodily sex morphology. Other similar terms sometimes used interchangeably are "bio" or "natal" male.

DHT—Dihydrotestosterone is an androgen hormone and primary contributing factor in male pattern baldness.

Fistula—a hole or opening in the skin (usually along a suture track) that fails to close properly. In genitoplasty for FTMs fistulas are complications usually associated with urethral lengthening and construction. Some fistulas heal on their own while others require surgical correction.

Foley Catheter—a tube passing through the urethra and into the bladder.

FTM—someone who is transitioning or has transitioned to a masculine or male gender identity from the female gender identity they were assigned at birth.

Gender dysphoria—discomfort with the gender category that one is assigned at birth and the gender roles associated with it. It may also entail a "felt" discomfort with one's morphological sex.

Genitoplasty—surgical alteration or (re)construction of any part of genitalia, external or internal. Also referred to as "genital, bottom, or lower surgery", "genital (re)construction" "sex reassignment surgery", and "sex/gender affirmation (or confirmation) surgery."

Glansoplasty—surgical construction of the head of penis

Hematoma—A pocket of blood accumulating outside the blood vessels. A complication associated with surgery in general.

Heteronormativity—the prescription of heterosexuality and gender binaries is the desired norms of sex and gender identity and expression.

Hysterectomy—surgical removal of the uterus and possible the cervix.

Laparoscopic—surgery conducted via minimal incisions using laparoscopes incision instruments with small cameras attached to them. The procedure is desirable for its minimal external scarring and build-up of scar tissue most commonly seen with scalpel surgery.

Metoidioplasty—surgical procedure releasing the clitoris by cutting the labial ligaments so that it protrudes more from the pubis mons.

MLD phalloplasty—a surgical method using the musculocutaneous latissimus dorsis flap from the back as donor tissue to create a penis.

Mons resection—removal of fatty tissue in the pubis mons (area surrounding the penis). This is usually done to enhance the phallic protrusion of metoidioplasty penises, allowing more access and giving more visibility to the penis.

MTF—someone who is transitioning or has transitioned to a feminine or female gender identity from the male gender they were assigned at birth.

Oophorectomy—surgical removal of one or more of the ovaries and possibly one or more of the fallopian tubes. This procedure is sometimes performed in conjunction with a hysterectomy.

Paracetamol—medication reducing fever.

Phalloplasty—surgical (re)construction of genitalia (internal and external) to form a penis.

Scrotoplasty—surgical (re)construction of a scrotum from the labia majora or tissue donated from another site. Usually includes testicular implants.

Supra-pubic catheter—a tube inserted directly into the bladder through a small hole in the pubis mons or lower abdomen and bypassing the urethra.

Tramadol—medication used to reduce pain.

Transsexualism—when someone identifies with a sex/gender that differs from the sex/gender they were assigned at birth.

Vaginectomy/colpectomy—surgery that usually, but does not always include closing the vaginal canal. Vaginectomy removes all of the vaginal lining, including mucous glands. Colpectomy is a more recent invention that improves upon the vaginectomy, requiring less time and involving less blood loss, pain, and complications.

Strictures—the narrowing of a passage or canal usually resulting in blockage of some kind. Most commonly associated with urethral lengthening in urethraplasty.

17048320R00102